A Brief Account of the Rise and Progress of the People Called

Quakers

By William Penn

Table of Contents

Introduction

Reader, this following account of the people called Quakers, &c. was written in the fear and love of God: first, as a standing testimony to that ever blessed truth in the inward parts, with which God, in my youthful time, visited my soul, and for the sense and love of which I was made willing, in no ordinary way, to relinquish the honors and interests of the world. Secondly, as a testimony for that despised people, that God has in his great mercy gathered and united by his own blessed Spirit in the holy profession of it; whose fellowship I value above all worldly greatness. Thirdly, in love and honor to the memory of that worthy servant of God, George Fox, the first instrument thereof, and therefore styled by me--The great and blessed apostle of our day. As this gave birth to what is here presented to thy view, in the first edition of it, by way of preface to George Fox's excellent Journal; so the consideration of the present usefulness of the following account of the people called Quakers, by reason of the unjust reflections of some adversaries that once walked under the profession of Friends, and the exhortations that conclude it, prevailed with me to consent that it should be republished in a smaller volume; knowing also full well, that great books, especially in these days, grow burthensome, both to the pockets and minds of too many; and that there are not a few that desire, so it be at an easy rate, to be informed about this people, that have been so much every where spoken against:

but blessed be the God and Father of our Lord Jesus Christ, it is upon no worse grounds than it was said of old time of the primitive Christians, as I hope will appear to every sober and considerate reader. Our business, after all the ill usage we have met with, being the realities of religion, an effectual change before our last and great change: that all may come to an inward, sensible, and experimental knowledge of God, through the convictions and operations of the light and spirit of Christ in themselves; the sufficient and blessed means given to all, that thereby all may come savingly to know the only true God, and Jesus Christ whom he hath sent to enlighten and redeem the world: which knowledge is indeed eternal life. And that thou, reader, mayst obtain it, is the earnest desire of him that is ever thine in so good a work.

WILLIAM PENN.

Chapter 1

Containing a brief account of divers dispensations of God in the world, to the time he was pleased to raise this despised people, called Quakers.

Divers have been the dispensations of God since the creation of the world, unto the sons of men; but the great end of all of them, has been the renown of his own excellent name in the creation and restoration of man: man, the emblem of himself, as a God on earth, and the glory of all his works. The world began with innocency; all was then good that the good God had made: and as he blessed the works of his hands, so their natures and harmony magnified him their Creator. Then the morning stars sang together for joy, and all parts of his work said Amen to his law. Not a jar in the whole frame; but man in paradise, the beasts in the field, the fowl in the air, the fish in the sea, the lights in the heavens, the fruits of the earth; yea, the air, the earth, the water, and fire, worshipped, praised, and exalted his power, wisdom, and goodness. O holy sabbath! O holy day to the Lord!

But this happy state lasted not long; for man, the crown and glory of the whole, being tempted to aspire above his place, unhappily yielded, against command and duty, as well as interest and felicity, and so fell below it; lost the divine image, the wisdom, power, and purity he was made in; by which, being no longer fit for paradise, he was expelled that garden of God, his proper dwelling and residence, and was driven out, as a poor vagabond, from the presence of the Lord, to wander in the earth, the habitation of beasts.

Yet God that made him had pity on him; for he, seeing man was deceived, and that it was not of malice, or an original presumption in him, but through the subtilty of the serpent, who had first fallen from his own state, and by the mediation of the woman, man's own nature and companion, whom the serpent had first deluded, in his infinite goodness and wisdom provided a way to repair the breach, recover the loss, and restore fallen man again by a nobler and more excellent Adam, promised to be born of a woman; that as by means of a woman the evil one had prevailed upon man, by a woman also he should come into the world, who would prevail against him, and bruise his head, and deliver man from his power: and which, in a signal manner, by the dispensation of the Son of God in the flesh, in the fulness of time was personally and fully accomplished by him, and in him, as man's Saviour and Redeemer.

But his power was not limited, in the manifestation of it to that time; for both before and since his blessed manifestation in the flesh, he has been the light and life, the rock and strength of all that ever feared God; was present with them in their temptations, followed them in their travels and afflictions, and supported and carried them through and over the difficulties that have attended them in their earthly pilgrimage. By this, Abel's heart excelled Cain's, and Seth obtained the pre-eminence, and Enoch walked with God. It was this that strove with the old world, and which they rebelled against, and which sanctified and instructed Noah to salvation.

But the outward dispensation that followed the benighted state of man, after his fall, especially among the patriarchs, was generally that of angels; as the scriptures of the Old Testament do in many places express, as to Abraham, Jacob, &c. The next was that of the law by Moses, which was also delivered by angels, as the apostle tells us. This dispensation was much outward, and suited to a low and servile state; called therefore, by the apostle Paul, that of a schoolmaster, which was to point out and prepare that people to look and long for the Messiah, who would deliver them from the servitude of a ceremonious and imperfect dispensation, by knowing the realities of those mysterious representations in themselves. In this time the law was written on stone, the temple built with hands, attended with an outward priesthood, and external rites and ceremonies, that were shadows of the good things that were to come, and were only to serve till the seed came, or the more excellent and general manifestation of Christ, to whom was the promise, and to all men only in him, in whom it was yea and amen, even life from death, immortality and eternal life.

This the prophets foresaw, and comforted the believing Jews in the certainty of it; which was the top of the Mosaical dispensation, which ended in John's ministry, the forerunner of the Messiah, as John's was finished in him, the fullness of all. And then God, that at sundry times, and in divers manners, had spoken to the fathers by his servants the prophets, spoke to men by his Son Christ Jesus, who is heir of all things, being the gospel-day, which is the dispensation of sonship: bringing in thereby a nearer testament, and a better hope; even the beginning of the glory of the latter days, and of the restitution of all things; yea, the restoration of the kingdom unto Israel.

Now the spirit, that was more sparingly communicated in former dispensations, began to be poured forth upon all flesh, according to the prophet Joel; and the light that shined in darkness, or but dimly before, the most gracious God caused to shine out of darkness, and the day-star began to rise in the hearts of believers, giving unto them the knowledge of God in the face, or appearance, of his Son Christ Jesus.

Now the poor in spirit, the meek, the true mourners, the hungry and thirsty after righteousness, the peacemakers, the pure in heart, the merciful and persecuted, came more especially in remembrance before the Lord, and were sought out and blessed by Israel's true Shepherd. Old Jerusalem with her children grew out of date, and the new Jerusalem into request, the mother of the sons of the gospel-day. Wherefore, no more at old Jerusalem, nor at the mountain of Samaria, will God be worshipped above other places; for, behold, he is, by his own Son, declared and preached a Spirit, and that he will be known as such, and worshipped in the spirit and in the truth. He will now come nearer than of old time, and he will write his law in the heart, and put his fear and spirit in the inward parts, according to his promise. Then signs, types, and shadows flew away, the day having discovered their insufficiency in not reaching to the inside of the cup, to the cleansing of the conscience; and all elementary services expired in and by him, that is the substance of all.

And to this great and blessed end of the dispensation of the Son of God, did the apostles testify, whom he had chosen and anointed by his spirit, to turn the Jews from their prejudice and superstition, and the Gentiles from their vanity and idolatry, to Christ's light and spirit that shined in them; that they might be quickened from the sins and trespasses in which they were dead, to serve the living God, in the newness of the spirit of life, and walk as children of the light, and of the day, even the day of holiness: for such put on Christ, the light of the world, and make no more provision for the flesh, to fulfill the lusts thereof. So that the light, spirit, and grace, that come by Christ, and appear in man, were that divine principle the apostles ministered from, and turned people's minds unto, and in which they gathered and built up the church of Christ in their day. For which cause they advise them not to quench the spirit, but to wait for the spirit, and speak by the spirit, and pray by the spirit, and walk in the spirit too, as that which approved them the truly begotten children of God, born not of flesh and blood, or of the will of man, but of the will of God; by doing his will, and denying their own; by drinking of Christ's cup, and being baptized with his baptism of self-denial; the way and path that all the heirs of life have ever trod to blessedness.

But alas! even in the apostles' days, those bright stars of the first magnitude of the gospel light, some clouds, foretelling an eclipse of this primitive glory, began to appear; and several of them gave early caution of it to the Christians of their time, that even then there was, and yet would be more and more, a falling away from the power of godliness, and the purity of that spiritual dispensation, by such as sought to make a fair show in the flesh, but with whom the offence of the cross ceased. Yet with this comfortable conclusion, that they saw beyond it a more glorious time than ever to the true church. Their sight was true; and what they foretold to the churches, gathered by them in the name and power of Jesus, came to pass: for Christians degenerated apace into outsides, as days, and meats, and divers other ceremonies. And, which was worse, they fell into strife and contention about them; separating one from another, then envying, and, as they had power, persecuting one another, to the shame and scandal of their common Christianity, and grievous stumbling and offence of the heathen; among whom the Lord had so long and so marvelously preserved them. And having got at last the worldly power into their hands, by kings and emperors embracing the Christian profession, they changed, what they could, the kingdom of Christ, which is not of this world, into a worldly kingdom; or, at least, styled the worldly kingdom that was in their hands, the kingdom of Christ, and so they became worldly and not true Christians. Then human inventions and novelties, both in doctrine and worship, crowded fast into the church; a door opened thereunto, by the grossness and carnality that appeared then among the generality of Christians, who had long since left the guidance of God's meek and heavenly spirit, and given themselves up to superstition, will-worship, and voluntary humility. And as superstition is blind, so it is heady and furious, for all must stoop to its blind and boundless zeal, or perish by it: in the name of the spirit, persecuting the very appearance of the spirit of God in others, and opposing that in others, which they resisted in themselves, viz. the light, grace, and spirit of the Lord Jesus Christ; but always under the notion of innovation, heresy, schism, or some such plausible name; though Christianity allows of no name, or pretense whatever, for persecuting of any man for matters of mere religion, being in its very nature meek, gentle, and forbearing; and consists of faith, hope, and charity, which no persecutor can have, whilst he remains a persecutor; in that a man cannot believe well, or hope well, or have a charitable or tender regard to another, whilst he would violate his mind, or persecute his body, for matters of faith or worship towards his God.

Thus the false church sprang up, and mounted the chair; but, though she lost her nature, she would needs keep her good name of the Lamb's bride, the true church, and mother of the faithful: constraining all to receive her mark, either in their forehead, or right-hand; that is, publicly, or privately. But, in deed and in truth, she was mystery Babylon, the mother of harlots, mother of those that, with all their show and outside of religion, were adulterated and gone from the spirit, nature, and life of Christ, and grown vain, worldly, ambitious, covetous, cruel, &c. which are the fruits of the flesh, and not of the spirit.

Now it was, that the true church fled into the wilderness, that is, from superstition and violence, to a retired, solitary, and lonely state: hidden, and as it were, out of sight of men, though not out of the world. Which shows, that her wonted visibility was not essential to the being of a true church in the judgment of the Holy Ghost; she being as true a church in the wilderness, though not as visible and lustrous, as when she was in her former splendor of profession. In this state many attempts she made to return, but the waters were yet too high, and her way blocked up; and many of her excellent children, in several nations and centuries, fell by the cruelty of superstition, because they would not fall from their faithfulness to the truth.

The last age did set some steps towards it, both as to doctrine, worship, and practice. But practice quickly failed: for wickedness flowed, in a little time, as well among the professors of the reformation, as those they reformed from; so that by the fruits of conversation they were not to be distinguished. And the children of the reformers, if not the reformers themselves, betook themselves, very early, to earthly policy and power, to uphold and carry on their reformation that had been begun with spiritual weapons; which I have often thought has been one of the greatest reasons the reformation made no better progress, as to the life and soul of religion. For whilst the reformers were lowly and spiritually minded, and trusted in God, and looked to him, and lived in his fear, and consulted not with flesh and blood, nor sought deliverance in their own way, there were daily added to the church such as, one might reasonably say, should be saved: for they were not so careful to be safe from persecution, as to be faithful and inoffensive under it: being more concerned to spread the truth by their faith and patience in tribulation, than to get the worldly power out of their hands that inflicted those sufferings upon them: and it will be well if the Lord suffer them not to fall, by the very same way they took to stand.

In doctrine they were in some things short; in other things, to avoid one extreme, they ran into another: and for worship, there was, for the generality, more of man in it than of God. They owned the spirit, inspiration, and revelation, indeed, and grounded their separation and reformation upon the sense and understanding they received from it, in the reading of the scriptures of truth. And this was their plea; the scripture is the text, the spirit the interpreter, and that to every one for himself. But yet there was too much of human invention, tradition, and art, that remained both in praying and preaching; and of worldly authority, and worldly greatness in their ministers; especially in this kingdom, Sweden, Denmark, and some parts of Germany. God was therefore pleased in England to shift us from vessel to vessel; and the next remove humbled the ministry, so that they were more strict in preaching, devout in praying, and zealous for keeping the Lord's day, and catechising of children and servants, and repeating at home in their families what they had heard in public. But even as these grew into power, they were not only for whipping some out, but others into the temple: and they appeared rigid in their spirits, rather than severe in their lives, and more for a party than for piety: which brought forth another people, that were yet more retired and select.

They would not communicate at large, or in common with others; but formed churches among themselves of such as could give some account of their conversion, at least of very promising experiences of the work of God's grace upon their hearts, and under mutual agreements and covenants of fellowship, they kept together. These people were somewhat of a softer temper, and seemed to recommend religion by the charms of its love, mercy, and goodness, rather than by the terrors of its judgments and punishments; by which the former party would have awed people into religion.

They also allowed greater liberty to prophesy than those before them; for they admitted any member to speak or pray, as well as their pastor, whom they always chose, and not the civil magistrate. If such found anything pressing upon them to either duty, even without the distinction of clergy or laity, persons of any trade had their liberty, be it never so low and mechanical. But alas! even these people suffered great loss: for tasting of worldly empire, and the favor of princes, and the gain that ensued, they degenerated but too much. For though they had cried down national churches and ministry, and maintenance too, some of them, when it was their own turn to be tried, fell under the weight of worldly honor and advantage, got into profitable parsonages too much, and outlived and contradicted their own principles; and, which was yet worse, turned, some of them, absolute persecutors of other men for God's sake, that but so lately came themselves out of the furnace; which drove many a step further, and that was into the water: another baptism, as believing they were not scripturally baptized: and hoping to find that presence and power of God, in submitting to this watery ordinance, which they desired and wanted.

These people also made profession of neglecting, if not renouncing and censuring not only the necessity, but use, of all human learning, as to the ministry; and all other qualifications to it, besides the helps and gifts of the spirit of God, and those natural and common to men. And for a time they seemed, like John of old, a burning and a shining light to other societies.

They were very diligent, plain, and serious; strong in scripture, and bold in profession; bearing much reproach and contradiction. But that which others fell by, proved their snare. For worldly power spoiled them too; who had enough of it to try them what they would do if they had more: and they rested also too much upon their watery dispensation, instead of passing on more fully to that of the fire and Holy Ghost, which was his baptism, who came with a fan in his hand, that he might thoroughly, and not in part only, purge his floor, and take away the dross and the tin of his people, and make a man finer than gold. Withal, they grew high, rough, and self-righteous; opposing further attainment; too much forgetting the day of their infancy and littleness, which gave them something of a real beauty; insomuch that many left them, and all visible churches and societies, and wandered up and down as sheep without a shepherd, and as doves without their mates; seeking their beloved, but could not find him, as their souls desired to know him, whom their souls loved above their chiefest joy.

These people were called Seekers by some, and the Family of Love by others; because, as they came to the knowledge of one another, they sometimes met together, not formally to pray or preach at appointed times or places, in their own wills, as in times past they were accustomed to do, but waited together in silence; and as anything rose in any one of their minds, that they thought savored of a divine spring, they sometimes spoke. But so it was, that some of them not keeping in humility, and in the fear of God, after the abundance of revelation, were exalted above measure; and for want of staying their minds in an humble dependance upon him that opened their understandings, to see great things in his law, they ran out in their own imaginations, and mixing them with those divine openings, brought forth a monstrous birth, to the scandal of those that feared God, and waited daily in the temple not made with hands, for the consolation of Israel; the Jew inward, and circumcision in spirit.

This people obtained the name of Ranters, from their extravagant discourses and practices. For they interpreted Christ's fulfilling of the law for us, to be a discharging of us from any obligation and duty the law required of us, instead of the condemnation of the law for sins past, upon faith and repentance: and that now it was no sin to do that which before it was a sin to commit; the slavish fear of the law being taken off by Christ, and all things good that man did, if he did but do them with the mind and persuasion that it was so. Insomuch that divers fell into gross and enormous practices; pretending in excuse thereof, that they could, without evil, commit the same act which was sin in another to do: thereby distinguishing between the action and the evil of it, by the direction of the mind, and intention in the doing of it. Which was to make sin super-abound by the aboundings of grace, and to turn from the grace of God into wantonness; a securer way of sinning than before: as if Christ came not to save us from our sins, but in our sins; not to take away sin, but that we might sin more freely at his cost, and with less danger to ourselves. I say, this ensnared divers, and brought them to an utter and lamentable loss as to their eternal state; and they grew very troublesome to the better sort of people, and furnished the looser with an occasion to profane.

Chapter 2

Of the rise of this People, their fundamental principle, and doctrine, and practice, in twelve points resulting from it: their progress and sufferings: an expostulation with England thereupon.

At was about that very time, as you may see in George Fox's annals, that the eternal, wise, and good God, was pleased, in his infinite love, to honor and visit this benighted and bewildered nation, with his glorious day-spring from on high; yea, with a more sure and certain sound of the word of light and life, through the testimony of a chosen vessel, to an effectual and blessed purpose, can many thousands say, glory be to the name of the Lord forever!

For as it reached the conscience, and broke the heart, and brought many to a sense and search, so that which people had been vainly seeking without, with much pains and cost, they, by this ministry, found within, where it was they wanted what they sought for, viz. the right way to peace with God. For they were directed to the light of Jesus Christ within them, as the seed and leaven of the kingdom of God; near all, because in all, and God's talent to all: a faithful and true witness, and just monitor in every bosom. The gift and grace of God to life and salvation, that appears to all, though few regard it. This the traditional Christian, conceited of himself, and strong in his own will and righteousness, overcome with blind zeal and passion, either despised as a low and common thing, or opposed as a novelty, under many hard names and opprobrious terms; denying, in his ignorant and angry mind, any fresh manifestations of God's power and spirit in man, in these days, though never more needed to make true Christians. Not unlike those Jews of old, that rejected the Son of God, at the very same time that they blindly professed to wait for the Messiah to come; because, alas! he appeared not among them according to their carnal mind and expectation.

This brought forth many abusive books, which filled the greater sort with envy, and lesser with rage; and made the way and progress of this blessed testimony straight and narrow, indeed, to those that received it. However, God owned his own work, and this testimony did effectually reach, gather, comfort, and establish the weary and heavy-laden, the hungry and thirsty, the poor and needy, the mournful and sick of many maladies, that had spent all upon physicians of no value, and waited for relief from heaven, help only from above; seeing, upon a serious trial of all things, nothing else would do but Christ himself; the light of his countenance, a touch of his garment, and help from his hand, who cured the poor woman's issue, raised the centurion's servant, the widow's son, the ruler's daughter, and Peter's mother: and like her they no sooner felt his power and efficacy upon their souls, but they gave up to obey him in a testimony to his power: and that with resigned wills and faithful hearts, through all mockings, contradictions, confiscations, beatings, prisons, and many other jeopardies that attended them for his blessed name's sake.

And, truly, they were very many, and very great; so that in all human probability they must have been swallowed up quick of the proud and boisterous waves that swelled and beat against them, but that the God of all their tender mercies was with them in his glorious authority; so that the hills often fled, and the mountains melted before the power that filled them; working mightily for them, as well as in them; one ever following the other. By which they saw plainly, to their exceeding great confirmation and comfort, that all things were possible with him with whom they had to do. And that the more that which God required seemed to cross man's wisdom, and expose them to man's wrath, the more God appeared to help and carry them through all to his glory.

Insomuch, that if ever any people could say in truth, Thou art our sun and our shield, our rock and sanctuary; and by thee we have leaped over a wall, and by thee we have run through a troop, and by thee we have put the armies of the aliens to flight; these people had a right to say it. And as God had delivered their souls of the wearisome burdens of sin and vanity, and enriched their poverty of spirit, and satisfied their great hunger and thirst after eternal righteousness, and filled them with the good things of his own house, and made them stewards of his manifold gifts; so they went forth to all quarters of these nations, to declare to the inhabitants thereof, what God had done for them; what they had found, and where and how they had found it, viz.--The way to peace with God: inviting all to come and see, and taste for themselves, the truth of what they declared unto them.

And as their testimony was to the principle of God in man, the precious pearl and leaven of the kingdom, as the only blessed means appointed of God to quicken, convince, and sanctify man; so they opened to them what it was in itself, and what it was given to them for; how they might know it from their own spirit, and that of the subtle appearance of the evil one: and what it would do for all those whose minds should be turned off from the vanity of the world, and its lifeless ways and teachers, and adhere to his blessed light in themselves, which discovers and condemns sin in all its appearances, and shows how to overcome it, if minded and obeyed in its holy manifestations and convictions: giving power to such, to avoid and resist those things that do not please God, and to grow strong in love, faith, and good works. That so man, whom sin hath made as a wilderness, over-run with briers and thorns, might become as the garden of God, cultivated by his divine power, and replenished with the most virtuous and beautiful plants of God's own right-hand planting, to his eternal praise.

But these experimental preachers of glad tidings of God's truth and kingdom could not run when they list, or pray or preach when they pleased, but as Christ their Redeemer prepared and moved them by his own blessed Spirit, for which they waited in their services and meetings, and spoke as that gave them utterance; and which was as those having authority, and not like the dry, and formal Pharisees. And so it plainly appeared to the serious-minded, whose spiritual eye the Lord Jesus had in any measure opened: so that to one was given the word of exhortation, to another the word of reproof, to another the word of consolation, and all by the same Spirit, and in the good order thereof, to the convincing and edifying of many.

And, truly, they waxed strong and bold through faithfulness; and by the power and Spirit of the Lord Jesus became very fruitful; thousands, in a short time, being turned to the truth in the inward parts, through their testimony in ministry and sufferings: insomuch as, in most counties, and many of the considerable towns of England, meetings were settled; and daily there were added such as should be saved. For they were diligent to plant and to water, and the Lord blessed their labors with an exceeding great increase; notwithstanding all the opposition made to their blessed progress, by false rumours, calumnies, and bitter persecutions; not only from the powers of the earth, but from every one that listed to injure and abuse them: so that they seemed, indeed, to be as poor sheep appointed to the slaughter, and as a people killed all the day long.

It were fitter for a volume than a preface, but so much as to repeat the contents of their cruel sufferings; from professors as well as from profane, and from magistrates as well as the rabble: that it may be said of this abused and despised people, they went forth weeping, and sowed in tears, bearing testimony to the precious seed, even the seed of the kingdom, which stands not in words, the finest, the highest that man's wit can use; but in power, the power of Christ Jesus, to whom God the Father hath given all power in heaven and in earth, that he might rule angels above, and men below. Who empowered them, as their work witnesseth, by the many that were turned through their ministry, from darkness to light, and out of the broad into the narrow way of life and peace: bringing people to a weighty, serious, and God-like conversation; the practice of that doctrine which they taught.

And as without this secret divine power, there is no quickening and regenerating of dead souls, so the want of this generating and begetting power and life, is the cause of the little fruit that the many ministries, that have been and are in the world, bring forth. O that both ministers and people were sensible of this! My soul is often troubled for them, and sorrow and mourning compass me about for their sakes. O that they were wise! O that they would consider, and lay to heart the things that truly and substantially make for their lasting peace!

Two things are to be considered; the doctrine they taught, and the example they led among all people. I have already touched upon their fundamental principle, which is as the corner-stone of their fabric: and, indeed, to speak eminently and properly, their characteristic, or main distinguishing point or principle, viz. the light of Christ within, as God's gift for man's salvation. This, I say, is as the root of the goodly tree of doctrines that grew and branched out from it, which I shall now mention in their natural and experimental order.

First, repentance from dead works to serve the living God. Which comprehends three operations. First, a sight of sin. Secondly, a sense and godly sorrow for sin. Thirdly, an amendment for the time to come. This was the repentance they preached and pressed, and a natural result from the principle they turned all people unto. For of light came sight; and of sight came sense and sorrow; and of sense and sorrow came amendment of life. Which doctrine of repentance leads to justification; that is, forgiveness of the sins that are past, through Christ the alone propitiation, and the sanctification or purgation, of the soul from the defiling nature and habits of sin present, by the Spirit of Christ in the soul; which is justification in the complete sense of that word: comprehending both justification from the guilt of the sins that are past, as if they had never been committed, through the love and mercy of God in Christ Jesus; and the creature's being made inwardly just, through the cleansing and sanctifying power and Spirit of Christ revealed in the soul; which is commonly called sanctification. But none can come to know Christ to be their sacrifice, that reject him as their sanctifier: the end of his coming being to save his people from the nature and defilement, as well as guilt of sin; and, therefore, those that resist his light and Spirit, make his coming and offering of none effect to them.

From hence sprang a second doctrine they were led to declare, as the mark of the prize of the high calling to all true Christians, viz. Perfection from sin, according to the scriptures of truth; which testify it to be the end of Christ's coming, and the nature of his kingdom, and for which his Spirit was and is given, viz. to be perfect as our Heavenly Father is perfect, and holy, because God is holy. And this the apostles labored for, that the Christians should be sanctified throughout in body, soul, and spirit; but they never held a perfection in wisdom and glory in this life, or from natural infirmities, or death, as some have, with a weak or ill mind, imagined and insinuated against them.

This they called a redeemed state, regeneration, or the new birth: teaching everywhere, according to their foundation, that unless this work was known, there was no inheriting of the kingdom of God.

Thirdly, this leads to an acknowledgment of eternal rewards and punishments, as they have good reason; for else, of all people, certainly they must be most miserable, who, for above forty years, have been exceeding great sufferers for their profession; and, in some cases, treated worse than the worst of men; yea, as the refuse and off-scouring of all things.

This was the purport of their doctrine and ministry; which for the most part, is what other professors of Christianity pretend to hold in words and forms, but not in the power of godliness; which, generally speaking, has been long lost by men's departing from that principle and seed of life that is in man, and which man has not regarded, but lost the sense of; and in and by which he can only be quickened in his mind to serve the living God in newness of life. For as the life of religion was lost, and the generality lived and worshipped God after their own wills, and not after the will of God, nor the mind of Christ, which stood in the works and fruits of the Holy Spirit; so that which these pressed, was not notion, but experience; not formality, but godliness; as being sensible in themselves, through the work of God's righteous judgments, that without holiness no man shall ever see the Lord with comfort.

Besides these general doctrines, as the larger branches, there sprang forth several particular doctrines, that did exemplify and farther explain the truth and efficacy of the general doctrine before observed, in their lives and examples. As,

I. Communion and loving one another. This is a noted mark in the mouths of all sorts of people concerning them: they will meet, they will help and stick one to another: whence it is common to hear some say, "Look how the Quakers love and take care of one another." Others, less moderate, will say, "The Quakers love none but themselves:" and if loving one another, and having an intimate communion in religion, and constant care to meet to worship God, and help one another, be any mark of primitive Christianity, they had it, blessed be the Lord, in an ample manner.

II. To love enemies. This they both taught and practised. For they did not only refuse to be revenged for injuries done them, and condemned it as of an unchristian spirit; but they did freely forgive, yea, help and relieve those that had been cruel to them, when it was in their power to have been even with them: of which many and singular instances might be given: endeavoring, through faith and patience, to overcome all injustice and oppression, and preaching this doctrine as Christian, for others to follow.

III. Another was, the sufficiency of truth-speaking, according to Christ's own form of sound words, of yea, yea, and nay, nay, among Christians, without swearing, both from Christ's express prohibition to swear at all; (Mat. v.) and for that, they being under the tie and bond of truth in themselves, there was no necessity for an oath; and it would be a reproach to their Christian veracity to assure their truth by such an extraordinary way of speaking; simple and uncompounded answers, as yea and nay, without asseveration, attestation, or supernatural vouchers, being most suitable to evangelical righteousness. But offering, at the same time, to be punished to the full for false-speaking, as others for perjury, if ever guilty of it: and hereby they exclude with all true, all false and profane swearing; for which the land did and doth mourn, and the great God was, and is, not a little offended with it.

IV. Not fighting, but suffering, is another testimony peculiar to this people: they affirm that Christianity teacheth people to beat their swords into plough-shares, and their spears into pruning-hooks, and to learn war no more; that so the wolf may lie down with the lamb, and the lion with the calf, and nothing that destroys be entertained in the hearts of people: exhorting them to employ their zeal against sin, and turn their anger against Satan, and no longer war one against another; because all wars and fightings come of men's own hearts' lusts, according to the apostle James, and not of the meek Spirit of Christ Jesus, who is captain of another warfare, and which is carried on with other weapons. Thus, as truth-speaking succeeded swearing, so faith and patience succeeded fighting, in the doctrine and practice of this people. Nor ought they for this to be obnoxious to civil government, since, if they cannot fight for it, neither can they fight against it; which is no mean security to any state. Nor is it reasonable, that people should be blamed for not doing more for others than they can do for themselves. And, Christianity set aside, if the costs and fruits of war were well considered, peace, with all its inconveniencies, is generally preferable. But though they were not for fighting, they were for submitting to government, and that, not only for fear, but for conscience-sake, where government doth not interfere with conscience; believing it to be an ordinance of God, and where it is justly administered, a great benefit to mankind. Though it has been their lot, through blind zeal in some, and interest in others, to have felt the strokes of it with greater weight and rigor than any other persuasion in this age; whilst they of all others, religion set aside, have given the civil magistrate the least occasion of trouble in the discharge of his office.

V. Another part of the character of this people was, and is, they refuse to pay tithes or maintenance to a national ministry; and that for two reasons: the one is, they believe all compelled maintenance, even to gospel-ministers, to be unlawful, because expressly contrary to Christ's command, who said, "Freely you have received, freely give:" at least, that the maintenance of gospel-ministers should be free, and not forced. The other reason of their refusal is, because these ministers are not gospel ones, in that the Holy Ghost is not their foundation, but human arts and parts. So that it is not matter of humor or sullenness, but pure conscience towards God, that they cannot help to support national ministries where they dwell, which are but too much and too visibly become ways of worldly advantage and preferment.

VI. Not to respect persons, was, and is, another of their doctrines and practices, for which they were often buffeted and abused. They affirmed it to be sinful to give flattering titles, or to use vain gestures and compliments of respect. Though to virtue and authority they ever made a deference; but after their plain and homely manner, yet sincere and substantial way: well remembering the examples of Mordecai and Elihu; but more especially the command of their Lord and Master Jesus Christ, who forbade his followers to call men Rabbi, which implies Lord or Master; also the fashionable greetings and salutations of those times; that so self-love and honor, to which the proud mind of man is incident, in his fallen state, might not be indulged, but rebuked. And though this rendered their conversation disagreeable, yet they that will remember what Christ said to the Jews, "How can you believe which receive honor one of another?" will abate of their resentment, if his doctrine has any credit with them.

VII. They also used the plain language of Thee and Thou, to a single person, whatever was his degree among men. And, indeed, the wisdom of God was much seen in bringing forth this people in so plain an appearance. For it was a close and distinguishing test upon the spirits of those they came among; showing their insides, and what predominated, notwithstanding their high and great profession of religion. This among the rest sounded harsh to many of them, and they took it ill, forgetting the language they use to God in their own prayers, and the common style of the scriptures, and that it is an absolute and essential propriety of speech. And what

28

good, alas! had their religion done them, who were so sensibly touched with indignation for the use of this plain, honest, and true speech?

VIII. They recommended silence by their example, having very few words upon all occasions. They were at a word in dealing: nor could their customers, with many words, tempt them from it, having more regard to truth than custom, to example than gain. They sought solitude: but when in company, they would neither use, nor willingly hear unnecessary or unlawful discourses: whereby they preserved their minds pure and undisturbed from unprofitable thoughts, and diversions. Nor could they humor the custom of Good Night, Good Morrow, God Speed; for they knew the night was good, and the day was good, without wishing of either; and that in the other expression, the holy name of God was too lightly and unthankfully used, and therefore taken in vain. Besides, they were words and wishes of course, and are usually as little meant, as are love and service in the custom of cap and knee; and superfluity in those, as well as in other things, was burthensome to them; and therefore, they did not only decline to use them, but found themselves often pressed to reprove the practice.

IX. For the same reason they forbore drinking to people, or pledging of them, as the manner of the world is: a practice that is not only unnecessary, but they thought evil in the tendencies of it, being a provocation to drink more than did people good, as well as that it was in itself vain and heathenish.

X. Their way of marriage is peculiar to them; and shows a distinguishing care above other societies professing Christianity. They say, that marriage is an ordinance of God, and that God only can rightly join man and woman in marriage. Therefore, they use neither priest nor magistrate; but the man and woman concerned take each other as husband and wife, in the presence of divers credible witnesses, promising to each other, with God's assistance, to be loving and faithful in that relation, till death shall separate them. But antecedent to this, they first present themselves to the monthly meeting for the affairs of the church where they reside; there declaring their intentions to take one another as husband and wife, if the said meeting have nothing material to object against it. They are constantly asked the necessary questions, [1] as in case of parents or guardians, if they have acquainted them with their intention, and have their consent, &c. The method of the meeting is, to take a minute thereof, and to appoint proper persons to inquire of their conversation and clearness from all others, and whether they have discharged their duty to their parents or guardians; and to make report thereof to the next monthly meeting, where the same parties are desired to give their attendance. [2] In case it appears they have proceeded orderly, the meeting passes their proposal, and so records it in their meeting book. And in case the woman be a widow, and hath children, due care is there taken that provision also be made by her for the orphans, before the meeting pass the proposals of marriage: advising the parties concerned, to appoint a convenient time and place, and to give fitting notice to their relations, and such friends and neighbors, as they desire should be the witnesses of their marriage: where they take one another by the hand, and by name promise reciprocally, love and fidelity, after the manner

30

before expressed. Of all which proceedings, a narrative in way of certificate is made, to which the said parties first set their hands, thereby confirming it as their act and deed; and then divers relations, spectators, and auditors, set their names as witnesses of what they said and signed. And this certificate is afterward registered in the record belonging to the meeting, where the marriage is solemnized. Which regular method has been, as it deserves, adjudged in courts of law a good marriage, where it has been by cross and ill people disputed and contested, for want of the accustomed formalities of priest and ring, &c.--ceremonies they have refused, not out of humor, but conscience reasonably grounded; inasmuch as no scripture example tells us, that the priest had any other part, of old time, than that of a witness among the rest, before whom the Jews used to take one another: and, therefore, this people look upon it as an imposition, to advance the power and profits of the clergy: and for the use of the ring, it is enough to say, that it was a heathenish and vain custom, and never in practice among the people of God, Jews, or primitive Christians. The words of the usual form, as "with my body I thee worship," &c. are hardly defensible. In short, they are more careful, exact, and regular, than any form now used; and it is free of the inconveniences, with which other methods are attended; their care and checks being so many, and such, as that no clandestine marriages can be performed among them.

XI. It may not be unfit to say something here of their births and burials, which make up so much of the pomp of too many called Christians. For births, the parents name their own children; which is usually some days after they are born, in the presence of the midwife, if she can be there, and those that were at the birth, who afterwards sign a certificate for that purpose prepared, of the birth and name of the child or children; which is recorded in a proper book, in the monthly-meeting to which the parents belong; avoiding the accustomed ceremonies and festivals.

XII. Their burials are performed with the same simplicity. If the body of the deceased be near any public meeting-place, it is usually carried thither, for the more convenient reception of those that accompany it to the burying-ground. And it so falls out sometimes, that while the meeting is gathering for the burial, [3] some or other has a word of exhortation, for the sake of the people there met together. After which the body is borne away by young men, or else those that are of their neighborhood, or those that were most of the intimacy of the deceased party: the corpse being in a plain coffin, without any covering or furniture upon it. At the ground they pause some time before they put the body into its grave, that if any there should have anything upon them to exhort the people, they may not be disappointed; and that the relations may the more retiredly and solemnly take the last leave of the body of their departed kindred, and the spectators have a sense of mortality, by the occasion then given them, to reflect upon their own latter end. Otherwise, they have no set rites or ceremonies on those occasions. Neither do the kindred of the deceased ever wear mourning; [4] they looking upon it as a worldly ceremony and piece of pomp; and that what mourning is fit for a Christian to have, at the departure of a beloved relation or friend, should be worn in the mind, which is only sensible of the loss: and the love they had to them, and remembrance of them, to be outwardly expressed by a respect to their advice, and care of those they have left behind them, and their love of that they loved. Which conduct of theirs, though unmodish or unfashionable, leaves nothing of the substance of things neglected or undone; and as they aim at no more, so that simplicity of life is what they observe with great satisfaction; though it sometimes happens not to be without the mockeries of the vain world they live in.

These things gave them a rough and disagreeable appearance with the generality; who thought them turners of the world upside down, as, indeed, in some sense they were: but in no other than that wherein Paul was so charged, viz. To bring things back into their primitive and right order again. For these and such like practices of theirs were not the result of humor, or for civil distinction, as some have fancied; but a fruit of inward sense, which God through his holy fear, had begotten in them. They did not consider how to contradict the world, or distinguish themselves as a party from others; it being none of their business, as it was not their interest; no, it was not the result of consultation, or a framed design, by which to declare or recommend schism or novelty. But God having given them a sight of themselves, they saw the whole world in the same glass of truth; and sensibly discerned the affections and passions of men, and the rise and tendency of things; what it was that gratified the lust of the flesh, the lust of the eye, and the pride of life, which are not of the Father, but of the world. And from thence sprang, in the night of darkness and apostasy, which hath been over people through their degeneration from the light and Spirit of God, these and many other vain customs, which are seen, by the heavenly day of Christ that dawns in the soul, to be either wrong in their original, or, by time and abuse, hurtful in their practice. And though these things seemed trivial to some, and rendered these people stingy and conceited in such persons' opinion;

there was and is more in them, than they were, or are, aware of.

It was not very easy to our primitive friends to make themselves sights and spectacles, and the scorn and derision of the world; which they easily foresaw must be the consequence of so unfashionable a conversation in it: but here was the wisdom of God seen in the foolishness of these things; first, that they discovered the satisfaction and concern that people had in and for the fashions of this world, notwithstanding their high pretences to another: in that any disappointment about them came so very near them, as that the greatest honesty, virtue, wisdom, and ability, were unwelcome without them. Secondly, it seasonably and profitably divided conversation; for this making their society uneasy to their relations and acquaintance, it gave them the opportunity of more retirement and solitude; wherein they met with better company, even the Lord God their Redeemer; and grew strong in his love, power, and wisdom; and were thereby better qualified for his service. And the success abundantly showed it, blessed be the name of the Lord.

And though they were not great and learned in the esteem of this world, (for then they had not wanted followers upon their own credit and authority,) yet they were generally of the most sober of the several persuasions they were in, and of the most repute for religion; and many of them of good capacity, substance, and account among men.

And also some among them wanted not for parts, learning, or estate; though then as of old, not many wise, or noble, &c, were called; or, at least, received the heavenly call, because of the cross that attended the profession of it in sincerity. But neither do parts or learning make men the better Christians, though the better orators and disputants; and it is the ignorance of people about the divine gift, that causes that vulgar and mischievous mistake. Theory and practice, speculation and enjoyment, words and life, are two things. O! it is the penitent, the reformed, the lowly, the watchful, the self-denying, and holy soul, that is the Christian! And that frame is the fruit and work of the Spirit, which is the life of Jesus; whose life, though hid in the fulness of it in God the Father, is shed abroad in the hearts of them that truly believe, according to their capacity. O that people did but know this to cleanse them, to circumcise them, to quicken them, and to make them new creatures indeed! recreated, or regenerated, after Christ Jesus unto good works; that they might live to God, and not to themselves; and offer up living prayers and living praises to the living God, through his own living Spirit, in which he is only to be worshipped in this gospel day.

O that they that read me could but feel me! for my heart is affected with this merciful visitation of the Father of lights and spirits to this poor nation, and the whole world through the same testimony. Why should the inhabitants thereof reject it? Why should they lose the blessed benefit of it? Why should they not turn to the Lord with all their hearts, and say from the heart, Speak Lord, for now thy poor servants hear: O that thy will may be done, thy great, thy good, and holy will, in earth as it is in heaven! do it in us, do it upon us, do what thou wilt with us; for we are thine, and desire to glorify thee our Creator, both for that, and because thou art our Redeemer; for thou art redeeming us from the earth, from the vanities and pollutions of it, to be a peculiar people unto thee. O! this were a brave day for England, if so she could say in truth! but alas, the case is otherwise! for which some of thine inhabitants, O land of my nativity! have mourned over thee with bitter wailing and lamentation. Their heads have been, indeed, as waters, and their eyes as fountains of tears, because of thy transgression and stiffneckedness; because thou wilt not hear, and fear, and return to the Rock, even thy Rock, O England! from whence thou art hewn. But be thou warned, O land of great profession, to receive him into thy heart. Behold, at that door it is he hath stood so long knocking; but thou wilt yet have none of him. O! be thou awakened! lest Jerusalem's judgments do swiftly overtake thee, because of Jerusalem's sins that abound in thee. For she abounded in formality, but made void the weighty things of God's law, as thou daily dost.

She withstood the Son of God in the flesh, and thou resistest the Son of God in the Spirit. He would have gathered her, as a hen gathereth her chickens under her wings, and she would not; so would he have gathered thee out of thy lifeless profession, and have brought thee to inherit substance; to have known his power and kingdom: for which he often knocked within, by his grace and Spirit; and without, by his servants and witnesses: but, on the contrary, as Jerusalem of old persecuted the manifestation of the Son of God in the flesh, and crucified him, and whipped and imprisoned his servants; so hast thou, O land! crucified to thyself afresh the Lord of life and glory, and done despite to his Spirit of grace; slighting the fatherly visitation, and persecuting the blessed dispensers of it by thy laws and magistrates: though they have early and late pleaded with thee in the power and Spirit of the Lord; in love and meekness, that thou mightest know the Lord, and serve him, and become the glory of all lands.

But thou hast evilly entreated and requited them, thou hast set at nought all their counsel, and wouldst have none of their reproof, as thou shouldst have had. Their appearance was too straight, and their qualifications were too mean for thee to receive them; like the Jews of old, that cried, Is not this the

Carpenter's Son, and are not his brethren among us; which of the scribes, of the learned (the orthodox) believe in him? Prophesying their fall in a year or two, and making and executing of severe laws to bring it to pass: endeavoring to terrify them out of their holy way, or destroy them for abiding faithful to it. But thou hast seen how many governments that rose against them, and determined their downfall, have been overturned and extinguished, and that they are still preserved, and become a great and a considerable people, among the middle sort of thy numerous inhabitants. And notwithstanding the many difficulties without and within, which they have labored under, since the Lord God eternal first gathered them, they are an increasing people; the Lord still adding unto them, in divers parts, such as shall be saved, if they persevere to the end. And to thee, O England! were they, and are they lifted up as a standard, and as a city set upon a hill, and to the nations round about thee, that in their light thou mayst come to see light, even in Christ Jesus the light of the world, and, therefore, thy light and life too, if thou wouldst but turn from thy many evil ways, and receive and obey it. "For in the light of the Lamb must the nations of them that are saved walk," as the scripture testifies.

Remember, O nation of great profession! how the Lord has waited upon thee since the dawning reformation, and the many mercies and judgments by which he has pleaded with thee; and awake and arise out of thy deep sleep, and yet hear his word in thy heart, that thou mayst live.

Let not this thy day of visitation pass over thy head, nor neglect thou so great salvation as is this which is come to thy house, O England! for why shouldst thou die? O land that God desires to bless, be assured it is he that has been in the midst of this people, in the midst of thee, and not a delusion, as thy mistaken teachers have made thee believe. And this thou shalt find by their marks and fruits, if thou wilt consider them in the spirit of moderation.

Chapter 3

Of the Qualifications of their Ministry. Eleven marks that it is Christian.

I. They were changed men themselves, before they went about to change others. Their hearts were rent, as well as their garments; and they knew the power and work of God upon them. And this was seen by the great alteration it made, and their stricter course of life, and more godly conversation that immediately followed upon it.

II. They went not forth, or preached, in their own time or will, but in the will of God; and spoke not their own studied matters, but as they were opened and moved of his Spirit, with which they were well acquainted in their own conversion: which cannot be expressed to carnal men, so as to give them any intelligible account; for to such it is, as Christ said, like the blowing of the wind, which no man knows whence it cometh, or whither it goeth. Yet this proof and seal went along with their ministry, that many were turned from their lifeless professions, and the evil of their ways, to an inward and experimental knowledge of God, and a holy life, as thousands can witness. And as they freely received what they had to say from the Lord, so they freely administered it to others.

III. The bent and stress of their ministry was conversion to God; regeneration and holiness. Not schemes of doctrines and verbal creeds, or new forms of worship: but a leaving off in religion the superfluous, and reducing the ceremonious and formal part, and pressing earnestly the substantial, the necessary and profitable part to the soul; as all, upon a serious reflection, must and do acknowledge.

IV. They directed people to a principle in themselves, though not of themselves, by which all that they asserted, preached, and exhorted others to, might be wrought in them, and known to them, through experience, to be true; which is a high and distinguishing mark of the truth of their ministry, both that they knew what they said, and were not afraid of coming to the test. For as they were bold from certainty, so they required conformity upon no human authority, but upon conviction, and the conviction of this principle, which they asserted was in them that they preached unto: and unto that they directed them, that they might examine and prove the reality of those things which they had affirmed of it, as to its manifestation and work in man. And this is more than the many ministers in the world pretended to. They declare of religion, say many things true, in words, of God, Christ, and the Spirit; of holiness and heaven; that all men should repent and amend their lives, or they will go to hell, &c. But which of them all pretend to speak of their own knowledge and experience; or ever directed to a divine principle, or agent, placed of God in man, to help him; and how to know it, and wait to feel its power to work that good and acceptable will of God in them?

Some of them, indeed, have spoken of the spirit, and the operations of it to sanctification, and performance of worship to God; but where and how to find it, and wait in it, to perform our duty to God, was yet as a mystery to be declared by this farther degree of reformation. So that this people did not only in words, more than equally press repentance, conversion, and holiness, but did it knowingly and experimentally; and directed those, to whom they preached, to a sufficient principle; and told them where it was, and by what tokens they might know it, and which way they might experience the power and efficacy of it to their souls' happiness. Which is more than theory and speculation, upon which most other ministers depend: for here is certainty; a bottom upon which man may boldly appear before God in the great day of account.

V. They reached to the inward state and condition of people; which is an evidence of the virtue of their principle, and of their ministering from it, and not from their own imaginations, glosses, or comments upon scripture. For nothing reaches the heart, but what is from the heart; or pierces the conscience, but what comes from a living conscience; insomuch as it hath often happened, where people have under secrecy revealed their state or condition to some choice friends, for advice or ease, they have been so particularly directed in the ministry of this people, that they have challenged their friends with discovering their secrets, and telling their preachers their cases, to whom a word hath not been spoken. Yea, the very thoughts and purposes of the hearts of many have been so plainly detected, that they have, like Nathaniel, cried out, of this inward appearance of Christ, "Thou art the Son of God, thou art the King of Israel." And those that have embraced this divine principle, have found this mark of its truth and divinity, that the woman of Samaria did of Christ when in the flesh, to be the Messiah, viz. It had told them all that ever they had done; shown them their insides, the most inward secrets of their hearts, and laid judgment to the line, and righteousness to the plummet; of which thousands can at this day give in their witness. So that nothing has been affirmed by this people, of the power and virtue of this heavenly principle, that such as have turned to it have not found true, and more; and that one half had not been told to them of what they have seen of the power, purity, wisdom, and goodness of God therein.

VI. The accomplishments, with which this principle fitted even some of the meanest of this people for their work and service, furnishing some of them with an extraordinary understanding in divine things, and an admirable, fluency, and taking-way of expression, gave occasion to some to wonder, saying of them, as of their Master, "Is not this such a mechanic's son, how came he by this learning?" As from thence others took occasion to suspect and insinuate they were Jesuits in disguise, who had the reputation of learned men for an age past; though there was not the least ground of truth for any such reflection; in that their ministers are known, the places of their abode, their kindred and education.

VII. That they came forth low, and despised, and hated, as the primitive Christians did; and not by the help of worldly wisdom or power, as former reformations in part have done: but in all things it may be said, this people were brought forth in the cross; in a contradiction to the ways, worships, fashions, and customs of this world; yea, against wind and tide, that so no flesh might glory before God.

VIII. They could have no design to themselves in this work, thus to expose themselves to scorn and abuse; to spend and be spent; leaving wife and children, house and land, and all that can be accounted dear to men, with their lives in their hands, being daily in jeopardy, to declare this primitive message revived in their spirits, by the good Spirit and power of God, viz.

That God is light, and in him is no darkness at all; and that he has sent his Son a light into the world, to enlighten all men in order to salvation; and that they that say they have fellowship with God, and are his children and people, and yet walk in darkness, viz. in disobedience to the light in their consciences, and after the vanity of this world, lie and do not the truth. But that all such as love the light, and bring their deeds to it, and walk in the light, as God is light, the blood of Jesus Christ his Son should cleanse them from all sin. Thus John i. 4. 19. Chap. iii. 20, 21. 1 John i. 5, 6, 7.

IX. Their known great constancy and patience in suffering for their testimony in all the branches of it; and that sometimes unto death, by beatings, bruisings, long and crowded imprisonments, and noisome dungeons: four of them in New England dying by the hands of the executioner, purely for preaching amongst that people: besides banishments, and excessive plunders and sequestrations of their goods and estates, almost in all parts, not easily to be expressed, and less to have been endured, but by those that have the support of a good and glorious cause; refusing deliverance by any indirect ways or means, as often as it was offered unto them.

X. That they did not only not show any disposition to revenge, when it was at any time in their power, but forgave their cruel enemies; showing mercy to those that had none for them.

XI. Their plainness with those in authority, like the ancient prophets, not fearing to tell them to their faces, of their private and public sins; and their prophesies to them of their afflictions and downfal, when in the top of their glory: also of some national judgments, as of the plague, and fire of London, in express terms; and likewise particular ones to divers persecutors, which accordingly overtook them; and were very remarkable in the places where they dwelt, which in time may be made public for the glory of God.

Thus, reader, thou seest this people in their rise, principles, ministry, and progress, both their general and particular testimony; by which thou mayst be informed how, and upon what foot, they sprang, and became so considerable a people. It remains next, that I show also their care, conduct, and discipline as a Christian and reformed society, that they might be found living up to their own principles and profession. And this the rather, because they have hardly suffered more in their character from the unjust charge of error, than by the false imputation of disorder: which calumny, indeed, has not failed to follow all the true steps that were ever made to reformation, and under which reproach none suffered more than the primitive Christians themselves, that were the honor of Christianity, and the great lights and examples of their own and succeeding ages.

Chapter 4

Of the discipline and practice of this people, as a religious society. The church power they own and exercise, and that which they reject and condemn: with the method of their proceedings against erring and disorderly persons.

This people increasing daily both in town and country, a holy care fell upon some of the elders among them, for the benefit and service of the church. And the first business in their view, after the example of the primitive saints, was the exercise of charity; to supply the necessities of the poor, and answer the like occasions. Wherefore collections were early and liberally made for that and divers other services in the church, and intrusted with faithful men, fearing God, and of good report, who were not weary in well doing; adding often of their own in large proportions, which they never brought to account, or desired should be known, much less restored to them, that none might want, nor any service be retarded or disappointed.

They were also very careful, that every one that belonged to them, answered their profession in their behavior among men, upon all occasions; that they lived peaceably, and were in all things good examples. They found themselves engaged to record their sufferings and services: and in the case of marriage, which they could not perform in the usual methods of the nation, but among themselves, they took care that all things were clear between the parties and all others: and it was then rare, that any one entertained an inclination to a person on that account, till he or she had communicated it secretly to some very weighty and eminent friends among them, that they might have a sense of the matter; looking to the counsel and unity of their brethren as of great moment to them. But because the charge of the poor, the number of orphans, marriages, sufferings, and other matters, multiplied; and that it was good that the churches were in some way and method of proceeding in such affairs among them, to the end they might the better correspond upon occasion, where a member of one meeting might have to do with one of another; it pleased the Lord, in his wisdom and goodness, to open the understanding of the first instrument of this dispensation of life, about a good and orderly way of proceeding; who felt a holy concern to visit the churches in person throughout this nation, to begin and establish it among them: and by his epistles, the like was done in other nations and provinces abroad; which he also afterwards visited, and helped in that service, as shall be observed when I come to speak of him.

Now the care, conduct, and discipline, I have been speaking of, and which are now practised among this people, is as followeth.

This godly elder, in every county where he travelled, exhorted them that some, out of every meeting of worship, should meet together once in the month, to confer about the wants and occasions of the church. And, as the case required, so those monthly meetings were fewer or more in number in every respective county; four or six meetings of worship, usually making one monthly meeting of business. And accordingly, the brethren met him from place to place, and began the said meetings, viz. For the poor, orphans, orderly walking, integrity to their profession, births, marriages, burials, sufferings, &c. And that these monthly meetings should, in each county, make up one quarterly meeting, where the most zealous and eminent friends of the county should assemble to communicate, advise, and help one another, especially when any business seemed difficult, or a monthly meeting was tender of determining a matter.

Also that these several quarterly meetings should digest the reports of their monthly meetings, and prepare one for each respective county, against the yearly meeting, in which all quarterly meetings resolve; which is held in London: where the churches in this nation, and other nations [5] and provinces, meet by chosen members of their respective counties, both mutually to communicate their church affairs, and to advise, and be advised in any depending case, to edification. Also to provide a requisite stock for the discharge of general expenses for general services in the church, not needful to be here particularized. [6]

At these meetings any of the members of the churches may come, if they please, and speak their minds freely, in the fear of God, to any matter; but the mind of each quarterly meeting, therein represented, is chiefly understood, as to particular cases, in the sense delivered by the persons deputed, or chosen for that service by the said meeting.

During their yearly meeting, to which their other meetings refer in their order, and naturally resolve themselves, care is taken by a select number, for that service chosen by the general assembly, to draw up the minutes [7] of the said meeting, upon the several matters that have been under consideration therein, to the end that the respective quarterly and monthly meetings may be informed of all proceedings; together with a general exhortation to holiness, unity, and charity. Of all which proceedings in yearly, monthly, and quarterly meetings, due record is kept by some one appointed for that service, or that hath voluntarily undertaken it. These meetings are opened and usually concluded in their solemn waiting upon God, who is sometimes graciously pleased to answer them with as signal evidences of his love and presence, as in any of their meetings of worship.

It is further to be noted, that in these solemn assemblies for the churches' service, there is no one presides among them after the manner of the assemblies of other people; Christ only being their President, as he is pleased to appear in life and wisdom in any one or more of them, to whom, whatever be their capacity or degree, the rest adhere with a firm unity, not of authority, but conviction, which is the divine authority and way of Christ's power and Spirit in his people: making good his blessed promise, "that he would be in the midst of his, where and whenever they were met together in his name, even to the end of the world." So be it.

Now it may be expected, I should here set down what sort of authority is exercised by this people, upon such members of their society as correspond not in their lives with their profession, and that are refractory to this good and wholesome order settled among them: and the rather, because they have not wanted their reproach and sufferings from some tongues and pens, upon this occasion, in a plentiful manner.

The power they exercise, is such as Christ has given to his own people, to the end of the world, in the persons of his disciples, viz. To oversee, exhort, reprove, and, after long suffering and waiting upon the disobedient and refractory, to disown them, as any longer of their communion, or that they will stand charged with the behavior of such transgressors, or their conversation, until they repent. The subject matter about which this authority, in any of the foregoing branches of it, is exercised, is, first, in relation to common and general practice. And, secondly, about those things that more strictly refer to their own character and profession, and which distinguish them from all other professors of Christianity; avoiding two extremes upon which many split, viz. persecution and libertinism, that is, a coercive power to whip people into the temple; that such as will not conform, though against faith and conscience, shall be punished in their persons or estates; or leaving all loose and at large, as to practice; and so unaccountable to all but God and the magistrate. To which hurtful extreme, nothing has more contributed than the abuse of church power, by such as suffer their passion and private interests to prevail with them, to carry it to outward force and corporal punishment: a practice they have been taught to dislike, by their extreme sufferings, as well as their known principle for a universal liberty of conscience.

On the other hand, they equally dislike an independency in society:--an unaccountableness, in practice and conversation, to the rules and terms of their own communion, and to those that are the members of it. They distinguish between imposing any practice that immediately regards faith or worship, which is never to be done or suffered, or submitted unto; and requiring Christian compliance with those methods that only respect church-business in its more civil part and concern; and that regard the discreet and orderly maintenance of the character of the society as a sober and religious community. In short, what is for the promotion of holiness and charity, that men may practise what they profess, live up to their own principles, and not be at liberty to give the lie to their own profession without rebuke, is their use and limit of church power. They compel none to them, but oblige those that are of them to walk suitably, or they are denied by them: that is all the mark they set upon them, and the power they exercise, or judge a Christian society can exercise, upon those that are members of it.

The way of their proceeding against such as have lapsed or transgressed, is this. He is visited by some of them, and the matter of fact laid home to him, be it any evil practice against known and general virtue, or any branch of their particular testimony, which he, in common, professeth with them. They labor with him in much love and zeal, for the good of his soul, the honor of God, and reputation of their profession, to own his fault and condemn it, in as ample a manner as the evil or scandal was given by him; which, for the most part, is performed by some written testimony under the party's hand: and if it so happen, that the party prove refractory, and is not willing to clear the truth they profess, from the reproach of his or her evil doing or unfaithfulness, they, after repeated entreaties and due waiting for a token of repentance, give forth a paper to disown such a fact, and the party offending: recording the same as a testimony of their care for the honor of the truth they profess.

And if he or she shall clear their profession and themselves, by sincere acknowledgment of their fault, and godly sorrow for so doing, they are received and looked upon again as members of their communion. For as God, so his true people, upbraid no man after repentance.

This is the account I had to give of the people of God called Quakers, as to their rise, appearance, principles, and practices, in this age of the world, both with respect to their faith and worship, discipline and conversation. And I judge it very proper in this place, because it is to preface the journal of the first, blessed, and glorious instrument of this work, and for a testimony to him in his singular qualifications and services, in which he abundantly excelled in this day, and which are worthy to be set forth as an example to all succeeding times, to the glory of the most high God, and for a just memorial to that worthy and excellent man, his faithful servant and apostle to this generation of the world.

Chapter 5

Of the first instrument or person by whom God was pleased to gather this people into the way they profess. His name George Fox: his many excellent qualifications; showing a divine, and not a human power to have been their original in him. His troubles and sufferings both from without and within. His end and triumph.

I am now come to the third head or branch of my preface, viz. the instrumental author. For it is natural for some to say, Well, here is the people and work, but where and who was the man, the instrument? He that in this age was sent to begin this work and people? I shall, as God shall enable me, declare who and what he was; not only by report of others, but from my own long and most inward converse, and intimate knowledge of him; for which my soul blesseth God, as it hath often done: and I doubt not, but by that time I have discharged myself of this part of my preface, my serious readers will believe I had good cause so to do.

The blessed instrument of, and in this day of God, and of whom I am now about to write, was George Fox, distinguished from another of that name, by that other's addition of younger to his name, in all his writings; not that he was so in years, but that he was so in the truth: but he was also a worthy man, witness, and servant of God in his time.

But this George Fox was born in Leicestershire, about the year 1624. He descended of honest and sufficient parents, who endeavored to bring him up, as they did the rest of their children, in the way and worship of the nation: especially his mother, who was a woman accomplished above most of her degree in the place where she lived. But from a child he appeared of another frame of mind than the rest of his brethren; being more religious, inward, still, solid, and observing beyond his years, as the answers he would give, and the questions he would put, upon occasion, manifested, to the astonishment of those that heard him, especially in divine things.

His mother, taking notice of his singular temper, and the gravity, wisdom, and piety, that very early shined through him, refusing childish and vain sports, and company, when very young, was tender and indulgent over him, so that from her he met with little difficulty. As to his employment, he was brought up in country business, and as he took most delight in sheep, so he was very skilful in them; an employment that very well suited his mind in several respects, both for its innocency and solitude; and was a just emblem of his after ministry and service.

I shall not break in upon his own account, which is by much the best that can be given, and therefore desire what I can, to avoid saying anything of what is said already, as to the particular passages of his coming forth: but, in general, when he was somewhat above twenty, he left his friends, and visited the most retired and religious people in those parts; and some there were in this nation, who waited for the consolation of Israel, night and day; as Zacharias, Anna, and good old Simeon did of old time. To these he was sent, and these he sought out in the neighboring counties, and among them he sojourned till his more ample ministry came upon him. At this time he taught, and was an example of, silence, endeavoring to bring them from self-performances; testifying of, and turning them to, the light of Christ within them, and encouraging them to wait in patience, and to feel the power of it to stir in their hearts, that their knowledge and worship of God might stand in the power of an endless life, which was to be found in the light, as it was obeyed in the manifestation of it in man. For in the word was life, and that life is the light of men: life in the word, light in men; and life in men too, as the light is obeyed: the children of the light living by the life of the word, by which the word begets them again to God, which is the regeneration and new birth, without which there is no coming into the kingdom of God: and to which whoever comes, is greater than John; that is, than John's dispensation, which was not that of the kingdom, but the consummation of the legal, and fore-running of the gospel-times, the time of the kingdom. Accordingly several meetings were gathered in those parts; and thus his time was employed for some years.

In 1652, he being in his usual retirement, his mind exercised towards the Lord, upon a very high mountain in some of the higher parts of Yorkshire, as I take it, he had a vision of the great work of God in the earth, and of the way that he was to go forth in a public ministry, to begin it. He saw people as thick as motes in the sun, that should in time be brought home to the Lord, that there might be but one shepherd and one sheepfold in all the earth. There his eye was directed northward, beholding a great people that should receive him and his message in those parts. Upon this mountain he was moved of the Lord to sound out his great and notable day, as if he had been in a great auditory; and from thence went north, as the Lord had shown him. And in every place where he came, if not before he came to it, he had his particular exercise and service shown to him, so that the

Lord was his leader indeed. For it was not in vain that he travelled; God in most places sealing his commission with the convincement of some of all sorts, as well publicans as sober professors of religion. Some of the first and most eminent of those that came forth in a public ministry, and who are now at rest, were Richard Farnsworth, James Nayler, William Dewsberry, Thomas Aldam, Francis Howgil, Edward Burroughs, John Camm, John Audland, Richard Hubberthorn, T. Taylor, T. Holmes, Alexander Parker, Wm. Simson, William Caton, John Stubbs, Robert Withers, Thomas Low, Josiah Coale, John Burnyeat, Robert Lodge, Thomas Salthouse, and many more worthies, that cannot well be here named; together with divers yet living of the first and great convincement; who, after the knowledge of God's purging judgment in themselves, and some time of waiting in silence upon him, to feel and receive power from on high to speak in his name, (which none else rightly can, though they may use the same words,) felt its divine motions, and were frequently drawn forth, especially to visit the public assemblies, to reprove, inform, and exhort them: sometimes in markets, fairs, streets, and by the highway-side: calling people to repentance, and to turn to the Lord with their hearts as well as their mouths; directing them to the light of Christ within them, to see, examine, and consider their ways by, and to eschew the evil, and do the good and acceptable will of God. And they suffered great hardships for this their love and good-will; being often stocked, stoned, beaten, whipped, and imprisoned, though honest men, and of good report where they lived; that had left wives, children, and houses and lands to visit them with a living call to repentance. And though the priests generally set themselves to oppose them, and wrote against them, and insinuated most false and scandalous stories to defame them, stirring up the magistrates to suppress them, especially in those northern parts; yet God was pleased to fill them with his living power, and give them such an open door of utterance in his service, that there was a mighty convincement over those parts.

And through the tender and singular indulgence of judge Bradshaw, and judge Fell, and colonel West, in the infancy of things, the priests were never able to gain the point they labored for, which was to have proceeded to blood; and, if possible, Herod-like, by a cruel exercise of the civil power, to have cut them off, and rooted them out of the country. But especially judge Fell, who was not only a check to their rage in the course of legal proceedings, but otherwise upon occasion; and finally countenanced this people. For, his wife receiving the truth with the first, it had that influence upon his spirit, being a just and wise man, and seeing in his own wife and family a full confutation of all the popular clamours against the way of truth, that he covered them what he could, and freely opened his doors, and gave up his house to his wife and her friends; not valuing the reproach of ignorant or evil-minded people: which I here mention to his and her honor, and which will be, I believe, an honor and a blessing to such of their name and family, as shall be found in that tenderness, humility, love, and zeal for the truth and people of the Lord.

That house was for some years, at first especially, until the truth had opened its way into the southern parts of this island, an eminent receptacle of this people. Others, of good note and substance in those northern countries, had also opened their houses, together with their hearts, to the many publishers, that, in a short time, the Lord had raised to declare his salvation to the people; and where meetings of the Lord's messengers were frequently held, to communicate their services and exercises, and comfort and edify one another in their blessed ministry.

But lest this may be thought a digression, having touched upon this before, I return to this excellent man; and for his personal qualities, both natural, moral, and divine, as they appeared in his converse with the brethren, and in the church of God, take as follows:

I. He was a man that God endued with a clear and wonderful depth: a discerner of others' spirits, and very much a master of his own. And though that side of his understanding which lay next to the world, and especially the expression of it, might sound uncouth and unfashionable to nice ears, his matter was nevertheless very profound; and would not only bear to be often considered, but the more it was so, the more weighty and instructing it appeared. And as abruptly and brokenly as sometimes his sentences would seem to fall from him, about divine things, it is well known they were often as texts to many fairer declarations.

And indeed it showed, beyond all contradiction, that God sent him, in that no arts or parts had any share in the matter or manner of his ministry; and that so many great, excellent, and necessary truths, as he came forth to preach to mankind, had therefore nothing of man's wit or wisdom to recommend them. So that as to man he was an original, being no man's copy; and his ministry and writings show they are from one that was not taught of man, nor had learned what he said by study. Nor were they notional or speculative, but sensible and practical truths, tending to conversion and regeneration, and the setting up of the kingdom of God in the hearts of men: and the way of it was his work. So that I have many times been overcome in myself, and been made to say, with my

Lord and Master, upon the like occasion, "I thank thee, O Father, Lord of heaven and earth, that thou hast hid these things from the wise and prudent of this world, and revealed them to babes:" for, many times hath my soul bowed in an humble thankfulness to the Lord, that he did not choose any of the wise and learned of this world to be the first messenger in our age, of his blessed truth to men; but that he took one that was not of high degree, or elegant speech, or learned after the way of this world, that his message and work he sent him to do might come with less suspicion, or jealousy of human wisdom and interest, and with more force and clearness upon the consciences of those that sincerely sought the way of truth in the love of it. I say, beholding with the eye of my mind, which the God of heaven had opened in me, the marks of God's finger and hand visibly in this testimony, from the clearness of the principle, the power and efficacy of it, in the exemplary sobriety, plainness, zeal, steadiness, humility, gravity, punctuality, charity, and circumspect care in the government of church-affairs, which shined in his and their life and testimony, that God employed in this work, it greatly confirmed me that it was of God, and engaged my soul in a deep love, fear, reverence, and thankfulness for his love and mercy therein to mankind: in which mind I remain, and shall, I hope, through the Lord's strength, to the end of my days.

II. In his testimony or ministry, he much labored to open truth to the people's understandings, and to bottom them upon the principle and principal, Christ Jesus the light of the world; that by bringing them to something that was from God in themselves, they might the better know and judge of him and themselves.

III. He had an extraordinary gift in opening the scriptures. He would go to the marrow of things, and show the mind, harmony, and fulfilling of them, with much plainness, and to great comfort and edification.

IV. The mystery of the first and second Adam, of the fall and restoration, of the law and gospel, of shadows and substance, of the servant's and Son's state, and the fulfilling of the scriptures in Christ and by Christ the true light, in all that are his, through the obedience of faith, were much of the substance and drift of his testimonies: in all which he was witnessed to be of God: being sensibly felt to speak that which he had received of Christ, and was his own experience, in that which never errs nor fails.

V. But, above all, he excelled in prayer. The inwardness and weight of his spirit, the reverence and solemnity of his address and behavior, and the fewness and fulness of his words, have often struck even strangers with admiration, as they used to reach others with consolation. The most awful, living, reverent frame I ever felt or beheld, I must say, was his in prayer. And truly it was a testimony he knew and lived nearer to the Lord than other men; for they that know Him most, will see most reason to approach him with reverence and fear.

VI. He was of an innocent life, no busy-body, nor self-seeker: neither touchy nor critical: what fell from him was very inoffensive, if not very edifying. So meek, contented, modest, easy, steady, tender, it was a pleasure to be in his company. He exercised no authority but over evil, and that everywhere, and in all; but with love, compassion, and long-suffering. A most merciful man, as ready to forgive, as unapt to take or give an offence. Thousands can truly say, he was of an excellent spirit and savor among them, and because thereof, the most excellent spirits loved him with an unfeigned and unfading love.

VII. He was an incessant laborer: for in his younger time, before his many, great, and deep sufferings and travels had enfeebled his body for itinerant services, he labored much in the word and doctrine, and discipline, in England, Scotland, and Ireland, turning many to God, and confirming those that were convinced of the truth, and settling good order, as to church affairs, among them. And towards the conclusion of his travelling service, between the years 1671, and 1677, he visited the churches of Christ in the plantations of America, and in the United Provinces, and Germany, as his journal relates; to the convincement and consolation of many. After that time he chiefly resided in and about the city of London; and, besides his labor in the ministry, which was frequent and serviceable, he wrote much, both to them that are within, and those that are without, the communion.

But the care he took of the affairs of the church in general was very great.

VIII. He was often where the records of the business of the church are kept, and where the letters from the many meetings of God's people over all the world use to come: which letters he had read to him, and communicated them to the meeting, that is weekly [8] held for such services; and he would be sure to stir them up to answer them, especially in suffering cases, showing great sympathy and compassion upon all such occasions; carefully looking into the respective cases, and endeavoring speedy relief, according to the nature of them. So that the churches, or any of the suffering members thereof, were sure not to be forgotten, or delayed in their desires, if he was there.

IX. As he was unwearied, so he was undaunted in his services for God and his people; he was no more to be moved to fear than to wrath. His behavior at Derby, Lichfield, Appleby, before Oliver Cromwell, at Launceston, Scarborough, Worcester, and Westminster Hall, with many other places and exercises, did abundantly evidence it, to his enemies as well as his friends.

But as, in the primitive times, some rose up against the blessed apostles of our Lord Jesus Christ, even from among those that they had turned to the hope of the gospel, and became their greatest trouble; so this man of God had his share of suffering from some that were convinced by him; who, through prejudice or mistake, ran against him, as one that sought dominion over conscience, because he pressed, by his presence or epistles, a ready and zealous compliance with such good and wholesome things, as tended to an orderly conversation about the affairs of the church, and in their walking before men. That which contributed much to this ill work, was, in some, a begrudging of this meek man the love and esteem he had and deserved in the hearts of the people; and weakness in others, that were taken with their groundless suggestions of imposition and blind obedience.

They would have had every man independent, that as he had the principle in himself, he should only stand and fall to that, and nobody else: not considering that the principle is one in all; and though the measure of light or grace might differ, yet the nature of it was the same; and being so, they struck at the spiritual unity which a people, guided by the same principle, are naturally led into: so that what is an evil to one, is so to all; and what is virtuous, honest, and of good repute to one, is so to all, from the sense and savor of the one universal principle which is common to all, and which the disaffected also profess to be the root of all true Christian fellowship, and that spirit into which the people of God drink, and come to be spiritually-minded, and of one heart and one soul.

Some weakly mistook good order in the government of church affairs, for discipline in worship, and that it was so pressed or recommended by him and other brethren. And thereupon they were ready to reflect the same things that dissenters had very reasonably objected upon the national churches, that have coercively pressed conformity to their respective creeds and worships. Whereas these things related wholly to conversation, and the outward, and, as I may say, civil part of the church; that men should walk up to the principles of their belief, and not be wanting in care and charity. But though some have stumbled and fallen through mistakes, and an unreasonable obstinacy even to a prejudice; yet, blessed be God, the generality have returned to their first love, and seen the work of the enemy, that loses no opportunity or advantage by which he may check or hinder the work of God, and disquiet the peace of his church, and chill the love of his people to the truth, and one to another; and there is hope of divers of the few that yet are at a distance.

In all these occasions, though there was no person the discontented struck so sharply at, as this good man, he bore all their weakness and prejudice, and returned not reflection for reflection; but forgave them their weak and bitter speeches, praying for them, that they might have a sense of their hurt, and see the subtilty of the enemy to rend and divide, and return into their first love that thought no ill.

And truly, I must say, that though God had visibly clothed him with a divine preference and authority, yet he never abused it; but held his place in the church of God with great meekness, and a most engaging humility and moderation. For upon all occasions, like his blessed Master, he was a servant to all; holding and exercising his eldership in the invisible power that had gathered them, with reverence to the Head, and care over the body: and was received, only in that Spirit and power of Christ, as the first and chief elder in this age: who, as he was therefore worthy of double honor, so for the same reason it was given by the faithful of this day; because his authority was inward and not outward, and that he got it and kept it by the love of God, and power of an endless life. I write my knowledge, and not report; and my witness is true; having been with him for weeks and months together on divers occasions, and those of the nearest, and most exercising nature; and that by night and by day, by sea and by land; in this and in foreign countries; and I can say, I never saw him out of his place, or not a match for every service or occasion. For in all things he acquitted himself like a man, yea, a strong man, a new and heavenly-minded man, a divine and a naturalist, and all of God Almighty's making. I have been surprised at his questions and answers in natural things: that whilst he was ignorant of useless and sophistical science, he had in him the grounds of useful and commendable knowledge, and cherished it everywhere. Civil, beyond all forms of breeding, in his behavior: very temperate, eating little, and sleeping less, though a bulky person.

Thus he lived and sojourned among us: and, as he lived, so he died; feeling the same eternal power, that had raised and preserved him, in his last moments. So full of assurance was he, that he triumphed over death; and so even in his spirit to the last, as if death were hardly worth notice, or a mention: recommending to some of us with him, the despatch and dispersion of an epistle just before given forth by him to the churches of Christ throughout the world, and his own books: but, above all, Friends; and of all Friends, those in Ireland and America, twice over, saying, "Mind poor Friends in Ireland and America."

And to some that came in and inquired how he found himself, he answered, "Never heed, the Lord's power is over all weakness and death; the seed reigns, blessed be the Lord:" which was about four or five hours before his departure out of this world. He was at the great meeting near Lombard-street, on the first day of the week, and it was the third following about ten at night when he left us; being at the house of Henry Goldney, in the same court. In a good old age he went, after having lived to see his children's children in the truth to many generations. He had the comfort of a short illness, and the blessing of a clear sense to the last: and we may truly say, with a man of God of old, that being dead, he yet speaketh: and though now absent in body, he is present in spirit; neither time nor place being able to interrupt the communion of saints, or dissolve the fellowship of the spirits of the just. His works praise him, because they are to the praise of Him that wrought by him; for which his memorial is and shall be blessed. I have done, as to this part of my preface, when I have left this short epitaph to his name,--Many sons have done virtuously in this day; but, dear George, thou excellest them all.

Chapter 6

Containing five several exhortations: first, general, reminding this people of their primitive integrity and simplicity. Secondly, in particular, to the ministry. Thirdly, to the young convinced. Fourthly, to the children of Friends. Fifthly, to those that are yet strangers to this people and way, to whom this book, and that which it was preface to, in its former edition, may come. All the several exhortations accommodated to their several states and conditions: that all may answer the end of God's glory, and their own salvation.

And now, Friends, you that profess to walk in the way that this blessed man was sent of God to turn us into, suffer, I beseech you, the word of exhortation, as well fathers as children, and elders as young men. The glory of this day, and foundation of the hope that has not made us ashamed since we were a people, you know, is that blessed principle of light and life of Christ which we profess, and direct all people to, as the great and divine instrument and agent of man's conversion to God. It was by this that we were first touched, and effectually enlightened, as to our inward state; which put us upon the consideration of our latter end, causing us to set the Lord before our eyes, and to number our days, that we might apply our hearts to wisdom. In that day we judged not after the sight of the eye, or after the hearing of the ear; but according to the light and sense this blessed principle gave us, so we judged and acted, in reference to things and persons, ourselves and others; yea, towards God our Maker. For being quickened by it in our inward man, we could easily discern the difference of things, and feel what was right and what was wrong, and what was fit, and what not, both in reference to religion and civil concerns. That being the ground of the fellowship of all saints, it was in that our fellowship stood. In this we desired to have a sense of one another, acted towards one another, and all men; in love, faithfulness, and fear.

In feeling of the stirrings and motions of this principle in our hearts, we drew near to the Lord, and waited to be prepared by it, that we might feel drawings and movings before we approached the Lord in prayer, or opened our mouths in ministry. And in our beginning and ending with this, stood our comfort, service, and edification. And as we ran faster, or fell short in our services, we made burdens for ourselves to bear; finding in ourselves a rebuke instead of an acceptance; and, in lieu of "Well-done," "Who has required this at your hands?" In that day we were an exercised people, our very countenances and deportment declared it.

Care for others was then much upon us, as well as for ourselves; especially of the young convinced. Often had we the burden of the word of the Lord to our neighbors, relations, and acquaintance; and sometimes strangers also. We were in travail likewise for one another's preservation; not seeking, but shunning, occasions of any coldness or misunderstanding; treating one another as those that believed and felt God present; which kept our conversation innocent, serious, and weighty; guarding ourselves against the cares and friendships of the world. We held the truth in the Spirit of it, and not in our own spirits, or after our own wills and affections.

We were bowed and brought into subjection, insomuch that it was visible to them that knew us. We did not think ourselves at our own disposal, to go where we list, or say or do what we list, or when we list. Our liberty stood in the liberty of the Spirit of truth; and no pleasure, no profit, no fear, no favor, could draw us from this retired, strict, and watchful frame. We were so far from seeking occasions of company, that we avoided them what we could; pursuing our own business with moderation, instead of meddling with other people's unnecessarily.

Our words were few and savory, our looks composed and weighty, and our whole deportment very observable. True it is, that this retired and strict sort of life, from the liberty of the conversation of the world, exposed us to the censures of many, as humorists, conceited and self-righteous persons, &c.; but it was our preservation from many snares, to which others were continually exposed, by the prevalency of the lust of the eye, the lust of the flesh, and the pride of life, that wanted no occasions or temptations to excite them abroad in the converse of the world.

I cannot forget the humility and chaste zeal of that day. O! how constant at meetings, how retired in them; how firm to truth's life, as well as truth's principles; and how entire and united in our communion, as, indeed, became those that profess one head, even Christ Jesus the Lord.

This being the testimony and example the man of God before mentioned was sent to declare and leave amongst us, and we having embraced the same, as the merciful visitation of God to us, the word of exhortation, at this time, is that we continue to be found in the way of this testimony, with all zeal and integrity, and so much the more, by how much the day draweth near. And first, as to you my beloved and much honored brethren in Christ, that are in the exercise of the ministry: O! feel life in your ministry. Let life be your commission, your well-spring and treasury on all such occasions; else, you well know, there can be no begetting to God: since nothing can quicken or make people alive to God, but the life of God; and it must be a ministry in and from life, that enlivens any people to God. We have seen the fruit of all other ministries, by the few that are turned from the evil of their ways. It is not our parts, or memory, the repetition of former openings, in our own will and time, that will do God's work. A dry doctrinal ministry, however sound in words, can reach but the ears, and is but a dream at the best. There is another soundness that is soundest of all, viz. Christ the power of God. This is the key of David, that opens, and none shuts; and shuts and none can open: as the oil to the lamp, and the soul to the body, so is that to the best of words: which made Christ to say, "My words, they are Spirit, and they are life;" that is, they are from life, and therefore they make you alive, that receive them. If the disciples that had lived with Jesus, were to stay at Jerusalem till they received it; much more must we wait to receive before we minister, if we will turn people from darkness to light, and from Satan's power to God.

I fervently bow my knees to the God and Father of our Lord Jesus Christ, that you may always be like-minded; that you may ever wait reverently for the coming and opening of the word of life, and attend upon it in your ministry and service, that you may serve God in his Spirit. And be it little, or be it much, it is well; for much is not too much, and the least is enough, if from the motion of God's Spirit; and without it, verily, never so little is too much, because to no profit.

For it is the Spirit of the Lord immediately, or through the ministry of his servants, that teacheth his people to profit; and to be sure, so far as we take him along with us in our services, so far we are profitable, and no further. For if it be the Lord that must work all things in us for our salvation, much more is it the Lord that must work in us for the conversion of others. If therefore it was once a cross to us to speak, though the Lord required it at our hands, let it never be so to be silent, when he does not.

It is one of the most dreadful sayings in the book of God, "That he that adds to the words of the prophecy of this book, God will add to him the plagues written in this book." To keep back the counsel of God, is as terrible; "For he that takes away from the words of the book of this prophecy, God shall take away his part out of the book of life." And truly, it has great caution in it, to those that use the name of the Lord, to be well assured the Lord speaks; that they may not be found of the number of those that add to the words of the testimony of prophecy, which the Lord giveth them to bear; nor yet to mince or diminish the same, both being so very offensive to God.

Wherefore, Brethren, let us be careful, neither to out-go our guide, nor yet loiter behind him; since he that makes haste may miss his way, and he that stays behind lose his guide. For even those that have received the word of the Lord, had need wait for wisdom, that they may see how to divide the word aright: which plainly implieth, that it is possible for one that hath received the word of the Lord, to miss in the dividing and application of it; which must come from an impatiency of spirit, and a self-working, which makes an unsound and dangerous mixture, and will hardly beget a right-minded living people to God.

I am earnest in this, above all other considerations, as to brethren in the ministry, (well knowing how much it concerns the present and future state and preservation of the church of

Christ Jesus, that has been gathered and built up by a living and powerful ministry,) that the ministry be held, preserved, and continued in the manifestations, motions, and supplies of the same life and power, from time to time.

And wherever it is observed, that any do minister more from gifts and parts, than life and power, though they have an enlightened and doctrinal understanding, let them in time be advised and admonished for their preservation, because insensibly such will come to depend upon a self-sufficiency; to forsake Christ the living Fountain, and hew out unto themselves cisterns, that will hold no living waters: and, by degrees, such will come to draw others from waiting upon the gift of God in themselves, and to feel it in others, in order to their strength and refreshment, to wait upon them, and to turn from God to man again, and so make shipwreck of the faith once delivered to the saints, and of a good conscience towards God: which are only kept by that divine gift of life that begat the one, and awakened and sanctified the other in the beginning.

Nor is it enough, that we have known the divine gift, and in it have reached to the spirits in prison, and been the instruments of the convincing of others of the way of God, if we keep not as low and poor in ourselves, and as depending upon the Lord, as ever: since no memory, no repetitions of former openings, revelations, or enjoyments, will bring a soul to God, or afford bread to the hungry, or water to the thirsty, unless life go with what we say, and that must be waited for.

O that we may have no other fountain, treasure, or dependence! That none may presume at any rate to act of themselves for God, because they have long acted from God; that we may not supply want of waiting, with our own wisdom, or think that we may take less care and more liberty in speaking than formerly; and that where we do not feel the Lord by his power, to open us and enlarge us, whatever be the expectation of the people, or has been our customary supply and character, we may not exceed or fill up the time with our own.

I hope we shall ever remember, who it was that said, "Of yourselves you can do nothing;" our sufficiency is in him. And if we are not to speak our own words, or take thought what we should say to men in our defence, when exposed for our testimony; surely, we ought to speak none of our own words, or take thought what we shall say in our testimony and ministry, in the name of the Lord, to the souls of the people: for then, of all times, and of all other occasions, should it be fulfilled in us, "For it is not you that speak, but the Spirit of my Father that speaketh in you."

And, indeed, the ministry of the Spirit must and does keep its analogy and agreement with the birth of the Spirit: that as no man can inherit the kingdom of God, unless he be born of the Spirit; so no ministry can beget a soul to God, but that which is from the Spirit. For this, as I said before, the disciples waited before they went forth; and in this our elder brethren and messengers of God in our day, waited, visited, and reached to us; and having begun in the Spirit, let none ever hope or seek to be made perfect in the flesh: for what is the flesh to the Spirit, or the chaff to the wheat? And if we keep in the Spirit, we shall keep in the unity of it, which is the ground of true fellowship. For by drinking into that one Spirit, we are made one people to God, and by it we are continued in the unity of the faith, and the bond of peace. No envying, no bitterness, no strife, can have place with us. We shall watch always for good, and not for evil, one over another; and rejoice exceedingly, and not begrudge at one another's increase in the riches of the grace with which God replenisheth his faithful servants.

And Brethren, as to you is committed the dispensation of the oracles of God, which give you frequent opportunities, and great place with the people among whom you travel, I beseech you, that you would not think it sufficient to declare the word of life in their assemblies, however edifying and comfortable such opportunities may be to you and them: but, as was the practice of the man of God before mentioned, in great measure, when among us, inquire the state of the several churches you visit; who among them are afflicted or sick, who are tempted, and if any are unfaithful or obstinate; and endeavor to issue those things in the wisdom and power of God, which will be a glorious crown upon your ministry. As that prepares your way in the hearts of the people, to receive you as men of God, so it gives you credit with them to do them good by your advice in other respects; the afflicted will be comforted by you, the tempted strengthened, the sick refreshed, the unfaithful convicted and restored, and such as are obstinate, softened and fitted for reconciliation; which is clinching the nail, and applying and fastening the general testimony, by this particular care of the several branches of it, in reference to them more immediately concerned in it.

For though good and wise men, and elders too, may reside in such places, who are of worth and importance in the general, and in other places; yet it does not always follow, that they may have the room they deserve in the hearts of the people they live among; or some particular occasion may make it unfit for him or them to use that authority. But you that travel as God's messengers, if they receive you in the greater, shall they refuse you in the less? And if they own the general testimony, can they withstand the particular application of it in their own cases? Thus ye will show yourselves workmen indeed, and carry your business before you, to the praise of his name that hath called you from darkness to light, that you might turn others from satan's power unto God and his kingdom, which is within. And O that there were more of such faithful laborers in the vineyard of the Lord!--Never more need since the day of God.

Wherefore I cannot but cry and call aloud to you, that have been long professors of the truth, and know the truth in the convincing power of it, and have had a sober conversation among men; yet content yourselves only to know truth for yourselves, to go to meetings, and exercise an ordinary charity in the church, and an honest behavior in the world, and limit yourselves within those bounds; feeling little or no concern upon your spirits, for the glory of the Lord in the prosperity of his truth in the earth, more than to be glad that others succeed in such service. Arise ye in the name and power of the Lord Jesus! Behold how white the fields are unto harvest, in this and other nations, and how few able and faithful laborers there are to work therein! Your country-folks, neighbors, and kindred, want to know the Lord and his truth, and to walk in it. Does nothing lie at your door upon their account! Search and see, and lose no time, I beseech you, for the Lord is at hand.

I do not judge you; there is one that judgeth all men, and his judgment is true. You have mightily increased in your outward substance, may you equally increase in your inward riches, and do good with both, while you have a day to do good. Your enemies would once have taken what you had, from you, for his name's sake in whom you have believed; wherefore he has given you much of the world, in the face of your enemies. But O, let it be your servant, and not your master! your diversion rather than your business! let the Lord be chiefly in your eye, and ponder your ways, and see if God has nothing more for you to do: and if you find yourselves short in your account with him, then wait for his preparation, and be ready to receive the word of command, and be not weary of well-doing, when you have put your hand to the plough; and, assuredly, you shall reap, if you faint not, the fruit of your heavenly labor in God's everlasting kingdom.

And you, young convinced ones, be you entreated and exhorted to a diligent and chaste waiting upon God, in the way of his blessed manifestation and appearance of himself to you. Look not out, but within: let not another's liberty be your snare: neither act by imitation, but by sense and feeling of God's power in yourselves: crush not the tender buddings of it in your souls, nor over-run, in your desires and warmness of affections, the holy and gentle motions of it. Remember it is a still voice that speaks to us in this day, and that it is not to be heard in the noises and hurries of the mind; but is distinctly understood in a retired frame. Jesus loved and chose solitudes, often going to mountains, gardens, and sea sides, to avoid crowds and hurries: to show his disciples it was good to be solitary, and sit loose to the world. Two enemies lie near your states, imagination and liberty; but the plain, practical, living, holy truth, that has convinced you, will preserve you, if you mind it in yourselves, and bring all thoughts, inclinations, and affections, to the test of it, to see if they are wrought in God, or of the enemy, or of your ownselves: so will a true taste, discerning, and judgment, be preserved to you, of what you should do and leave undone. And in your diligence and faithfulness in this way, you will come to inherit substance; and Christ, the eternal wisdom, will fill your treasury. And when you are converted, as well as convinced, then confirm your brethren; and be ready to every good word and work, that the Lord shall call you to: that you may be to his praise, who has chosen you to be partakers, with the saints in light, of a kingdom that cannot be shaken, an inheritance incorruptible in eternal habitations.

And now, as for you that are the children of God's people, a great concern is upon my spirit for your good and often are my knees bowed to the God of your fathers for you, that you may come to be partakers of the same divine life and power, that have been the glory of this day: that a generation you may be to God, a holy nation, and a peculiar people, zealous of good works, when all our heads are laid in the dust. O! you young men and women, let it not suffice you, that you are the children of the people of the Lord; you must also be born again, if you will inherit the kingdom of God. Your fathers are but such after the flesh, and could but beget you into the likeness of the first Adam; but you must be begotten into the likeness of the second Adam, by a spiritual generation, or you will not, you cannot, be of his children or offspring. And therefore look carefully about you, O ye children of the children of God; consider your standing, and see what you are in relation to this divine kindred, family, and birth. Have you obeyed the light, and received and walked in the Spirit, which is the incorruptible seed of the word and kingdom of God, of which you must be born again? God is no respecter of persons. The father cannot save or answer for the child, or the child for the father; but in the sin thou sinnest thou shalt die; and in the righteousness thou doest, through Christ Jesus, thou shalt live: for it is the willing and obedient that shall eat the good of the land. Be not deceived, God is mocked. Such as all nations and people sow, such they shall reap at the hand of the just God. And then your many and great privileges, above the children of other people, will add weight in the scale against you, if you choose not the way of the Lord. For you have had line upon line, and precept upon precept, and not only good doctrine but good example; and which is more, you have been turned to, and acquainted with, a principle in yourselves, which others too generally have been ignorant of: and you know you may be as good as you please, without the fear of frowns and blows, or being turned out of doors, and forsaken of father and mother, for God's sake and his holy religion; as has been the case of some of your fathers in the day they first entered into this holy path. And if you, after hearing and seeing the wonders that God has wrought in the deliverance and preservation of them, through a sea of troubles, and the manifold temporal, as well as spiritual, blessings that he has filled them with, in the sight of their enemies, should neglect and turn your backs upon so great and near a salvation, you would not only be most ungrateful children to God and them, but must expect that God will call the children of those that knew him not, to take the crown out of your hands, and that your lot will be a dreadful judgment at the hand of the Lord: but, O that it may never be so with any of you! The Lord forbid, saith my soul.

Wherefore, O ye young men and women! look to the rock of your fathers: there is no other God but him, no other light but his, no other grace but his, nor spirit but his, to convince you, quicken, and comfort you; to lead, guide, and preserve you to God's everlasting kingdom. So will you be possessors as well as professors of the truth, embracing it, not only by education, but judgment and conviction; from a sense begotten in your souls, through the operation of the eternal Spirit and power of God; by which you may come to be the seed of Abraham, through faith, and the circumcision not

76

made with hands; and so heirs of the promise made to the fathers, of an incorruptible crown. That, as I said before, a generation you may be to God, holding up the profession of the blessed truth in the life and power of it. For formality in religion is nauseous to God and good men; and the more so, where any form or appearance has been new and peculiar, and begun and practised, upon a principle, with an uncommon zeal and strictness. Therefore I say, for you to fall flat and formal, and continue the profession, without that salt and savor by which it is come to obtain a good report among men, is not to answer God's love, or your parents' care, or the mind of truth in yourselves, or in those that are without: who, though they will not obey the truth, have sight and sense enough to see if they do that make a profession of it. For where the divine virtue of it is not felt in the soul, and waited for and lived in, imperfections will quickly break out, and show themselves, and detect the unfaithfulness of such persons; and that their insides are not seasoned with the nature of that holy principle which they profess.

Wherefore, dear children, let me entreat you to shut your eyes at the temptations and allurements of this low and perishing world, and not suffer your affections to be captivated by those lusts and vanities that your fathers, for the truth's sake, long since turned their backs upon: but as you believe it to be the truth, receive it into your hearts, that you may become the children of God: so that it may never be said of you, as the evangelist writes of the Jews in his time, that Christ, the true light, "came to his own, but his own received him not; but to as many as received him, to them he gave power to become the children of God; which were born, not of blood, nor of the will of the flesh, nor of the will of man, but of God;" a most close and comprehensive passage to this occasion. You exactly and peculiarly answer to those professing Jews, in that you bear the name of God's people, by being the children, and wearing of the form of God's people: and he, by his light in you, may be very well said to come to his own, and if you obey it not, but turn your backs upon it, and walk after the vanities of your minds, you will be of those that received him not; which I pray God may never be your case and judgment. But that you may be thoroughly sensible of the many and great obligations you lie under to the Lord for his love, and to your parents for their care: and with all your heart, and all your soul, and all your strength, turn to the Lord, to his gift and Spirit in you; and hear his voice, and obey it, that you may seal to the testimony of your fathers, by the truth and evidence of your own experience: that your children's children may bless you, and the Lord for you, as those that delivered a faithful example, as well as record of the truth of God unto them. So will the grey hairs of your dear parents, yet alive, go down to the grave with joy, to see you the posterity of truth, as well as theirs: and that not only their nature, but spirit, shall live in you when they are gone.

* * * * *

I shall conclude this account with a few words to those who are not of our communion, into whose hands this may come; especially those of our own nation.

* * * * *

Friends, as you are the sons and daughters of Adam, and my brethren after the flesh, often and earnest have been my desires and prayers to God on your behalf, that you may come to know your Creator to be your Redeemer, and Restorer to the holy image that through sin you have lost, by the power and Spirit of his Son Jesus Christ, whom he hath given for the light and life of the world. And O that you, who are called Christians, would receive him into your hearts! for there it is you want him, and at that door he stands knocking, that you might let him in; but you do not open to him; you are full of other guests, so that a manger is his lot among you now as well as of old. Yet you are full of profession, as were the Jews when he came among them, who knew him not, but rejected and evily entreated him. So that if you come not to the possession and experience of what you profess, all your formality and religion will stand you in no stead in the day of God's judgment.

I beseech you ponder with yourselves your eternal condition, and see what title, what ground and foundation you have for your Christianity: if more than a profession, and an historical belief of the gospel. Have you known the baptism of fire, and the Holy Ghost, and the fan of Christ that winnows away the chaff in your minds, the carnal lusts, and affections; that divine leaven of the kingdom, that, being received, leavens the whole lump of man, sanctifying him throughout in body, soul, and spirit? If this be not the ground of your confidence, you are in a miserable state.

You will say, perhaps, that though you are sinners, and live in daily commission of sin, and are not sanctified, as I have been speaking, yet you have faith in Christ, who has borne the curse for you, and in him you are complete by faith, his righteousness being imputed to you.

But, my friends, let me entreat you not to deceive yourselves, in so important a point, as is that of your immortal souls. If you have true faith in Christ, your faith will make you clean; it will sanctify you: for the saints' faith was their victory of old: by this they overcame sin within, and sinful man without. And if thou art in Christ, thou walkest not after the flesh, but after the Spirit, whose fruits are manifest. Yea, thou art a new creature: new made, new fashioned, after God's will and mould. Old things are done away, and, behold, all things are become new: new love, desires, will, affections, and practices. It is not any longer thou that livest; (thou disobedient, carnal, worldly one;) but it is Christ that liveth in thee; and to live is Christ, and to die is thy eternal gain: because thou art assured, that thy corruptible shall put on incorruption, and thy mortal, immortality, and that thou hast a glorious house, eternal in the heavens, that will never wax old or pass away. All this follows being in Christ, as heat follows fire, and light the sun.

Therefore have a care how you presume to rely upon such a notion, as that you are in Christ, whilst in your old fallen nature. For what communion hath light with darkness, or Christ with Belial? Hear what the beloved disciple tells you: "If we say we have fellowship with God, and walk in darkness, we lie, and do not the truth." That is, if we go on in a sinful way, are captivated by our carnal affections, and are not converted to God, we walk in darkness, and cannot possibly in that state have any fellowship with God. Christ clothes them with his righteousness, that receive his grace in their hearts, and deny themselves, and take up his cross daily, and follow him. Christ's righteousness makes men inwardly holy; of holy minds, wills, and practices. It is not the less Christ's, because we have it; for it is ours, not by nature, but by faith and adoption: it is the gift of God. But, still, though not ours, as of or from ourselves, (for in that sense it is Christ's, for it is of and from him,) yet it is ours, and must be ours, in possession, efficacy, and enjoyment, to do us any good; or Christ's righteousness will profit us nothing. It was after this manner that he was made to the primitive Christians, righteousness, sanctification, justification, and redemption; and if ever you will have the comfort, kernel, and marrow of the Christian religion, thus you must come to learn and obtain it.

Now, my friends, by what you have read, you may perceive that God has visited a poor people among you, with this saving knowledge and testimony, whom he has upheld and increased to this day, notwithstanding the fierce opposition they have met withal. Despise not the meanness of this appearance: it was, and yet is, we know, a day of small things and of small account with too many; and many hard and ill names are given to it; but it is of God, it came from him, because it leads to him. This we know, but we cannot make another to know it, unless he will take the same way to know it that we took. The world talks of God, but what do they do? They pray for power, but reject the principle in which it is. If you would know God, and worship and serve God as you should do, you must come to the means he has ordained and given for that purpose. Some seek it in books, some in learned men; but what they look for is in themselves, (though not of themselves,) but they overlook it. The voice is too still, the seed too small, and the light shineth in darkness; they are abroad, and so cannot divide the spoil: but the woman that lost her silver, found it at home, after she had lighted her candle, and swept her house. Do you so too, and you shall find what Pilate wanted to know, viz. Truth. Truth in the inward parts, so valuable in the sight of God.

The light of Christ within, who is the light of the world, and so a light to you, that tells you the truth of your condition, leads all, that take heed unto it, out of darkness into God's marvellous light. For light grows upon the obedient; it is sown for the righteous, and their way is a shining light, that shines forth more and more to the perfect day.

Wherefore, O friends, turn in, turn in, I beseech you: where is the poison, there is the antidote. There you want Christ, and there you must find him; and blessed be God, there you may find him. Seek and you shall find, I testify for God. But then you must seek aright, with your whole heart, as men that seek for their lives, yea for their eternal lives: diligently, humbly, patiently, as those that can taste no pleasure, comfort, or satisfaction in anything else, unless you find him whom your souls want to know and love above all. O it is a travail, a spiritual travail! let the carnal, profane world, think and say as it will. And through this path you must walk to the city of God, that has eternal foundations, if ever you will come there.

Well! and what doth this blessed light do for you? Why, first, it sets all your sins in order before you: it detects the spirit of this world in all its baits and allurements, and shows how man came to fall from God, and the fallen state he is in. Secondly, it begets a sense and sorrow, in such as believe in it, for this fearful lapse. You will then see him distinctly whom you have pierced, and all the blows and wounds you have given him by your disobedience, and how you have made him to serve with your sins; and you will weep and mourn for it, and your sorrow will be a godly sorrow. Thirdly, after this it will bring you to the holy watch, to take care that you do so no more, and that the enemy surprise you not again. Then thoughts, as well as words and works, will come to judgment, which is the way of holiness, in which the redeemed of the Lord do walk. Here you will come to love

God above all, and your neighbors as yourselves. Nothing hurts, nothing harms, nothing makes afraid on this holy mountain. Now you come to be Christ's indeed; for you are his in nature and spirit, and not your own. And when you are thus Christ's, then Christ is yours, and not before. And here you will know communion with the Father and with the Son, and the efficacy of the blood of cleansing, even the blood of Jesus Christ, that immaculate Lamb, which speaks better things than the blood of Abel; and which cleanseth from all sin, the consciences of those that, through the living faith, come to be sprinkled with it, from dead works to serve the living God.

* * * * *

To conclude; behold the testimony and doctrine of the people called Quakers; behold their practice and discipline; and behold the blessed man and men, at least many of them, that were sent of God in this excellent work and service; all which is more particularly expressed in the annals of that man of God, which I do heartily recommend to my reader's most serious perusal; and beseech Almighty God, that his blessing may go along with both, to the convincement of many, as yet strangers to this holy dispensation, and also to the edification of God's church in general: who for his manifold and repeated mercies and blessings to his people, in this day of his great love, is worthy ever to have the glory, honor, thanksgiving, and renown; and be it rendered and ascribed, with fear and reverence, through him in whom he is well pleased, his beloved Son and Lamb, our light and life, that sits with him upon the throne, world without end. Amen.

Says one that God has long since mercifully favored with his fatherly visitation, and who was not disobedient to the heavenly vision and call; to whom the way of truth is more lovely and precious than ever, and that knowing the beauty and benefit of it above all worldly treasures, has chosen it for his chiefest joy, and therefore recommends it to thy love and choice, because he is with great sincerity and affection,

Thy soul's friend,

WILLIAM PENN.

Footnotes

1. Instead of being asked those questions, the present practice is to produce the needful certificates of consent.

2. This second attendance is not now required.

3. This hardly describes the present practice. It is not during the gathering only, if at all, that exhortation takes place. If the corpse be conveyed to a meeting-house, the meeting is held like any other; and what is here called Exhortation,' takes place or not, as any minister present believes him or herself influenced. The usage at the burial ground is still as here described. Interments often take place without any previous meeting.

4. The collective sense and judgment of the church, herein, remains the same, as is manifest by the frequent advices given forth from their yearly and other meetings.

5. At present (1834) there are eight yearly meetings on the American continent, which correspond with the yearly meeting in London, and mutually with each other; they are united in doctrine, and their discipline is similar.

6. They are thus particularized in a more recent publication of the society:--This is an occasional voluntary contribution, expended in printing books; house-rent for a clerk, and his wages for keeping records; the passage of ministers who visit their brethren beyond sea; and some small incidental charges; but not, as has been falsely supposed, the

reimbursement of those who suffer distraint for tithes, and other demands, with which they scruple to comply.

7. This is not now quite correct. A committee still draws up the General Epistle; but the minutes of the transactions of the meeting are made as matters occur during its several sittings.

8. Called the Meeting for Sufferings, and now held monthly, except exigencies require more frequent sittings.

Made in the USA
Coppell, TX
02 August 2024